# HOW TEXTS WORK

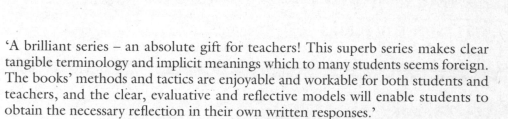

'A brilliant series – an absolute gift for teachers! This superb series makes clear tangible terminology and implicit meanings which to many students seems foreign. The books' methods and tactics are enjoyable and workable for both students and teachers, and the clear, evaluative and reflective models will enable students to obtain the necessary reflection in their own written responses.'

> Kesner Ridge, Hagley Roman Catholic High School, Worcestershire, and
> Outstanding New Teacher 2002 (*The Guardian Teaching Awards*)

'This is the series we've all been waiting for! Tightly focused on the assessment objectives, these books provide an excellent aid to classroom teaching and self-study. Whether your school changes board or text, or decides to offer Literature and/or Language to 6th formers these books are still the tool that can make a real difference to results.'

> Emmeline McChleery, Aylesford School, Warwick

*Routledge A Level English Guides* equip AS and A2 Level students with the skills they need to explore, evaluate, and enjoy English. What has – until now – been lacking for the revised English A Levels is a set of textbooks that equip students with the concepts, skills and knowledge they need to succeed in light of the way the exams are actually working. The *Routledge A Level English Guides* series fills this critical gap.

Books in the series are built around the various skills specified in the assessment objectives (AOs) for all AS and A2 Level English courses, and take into account how these AOs are being interpreted by the exam boards. Focusing on the AOs most relevant to their topic, the books help students to develop their knowledge and abilities through analysis of a wide range of texts and data. Each book also offers accessible **explanations**, **examples**, **exercises**, **summaries**, **suggested answers** and **a glossary of key terms**.

The series helps students to learn what is required of them and develop skills accordingly, while ensuring that English remains an exciting subject that students enjoy studying. The books are also an essential resource for teachers trying to create lessons which balance the demands of the exam boards with the more general skills and knowledge students need for the critical appreciation of English Language and Literature.

# ROUTLEDGE A LEVEL ENGLISH GUIDES

## About the Series Editor

**Adrian Beard** was Head of English at Gosforth High School, Newcastle upon Tyne. He now works at the University of Newcastle upon Tyne and is a Chief Examiner for AS and A2 Level English Literature. He is co-series editor of the Routledge Intertext series, and his publications include *Texts and Contexts*, *The Language of Politics*, and *The Language of Sport* (all for Routledge).

## TITLES IN THE SERIES

*The Language of Literature*
Adrian Beard

*How Texts Work*
Adrian Beard

*Language and Social Contexts*
Amanda Coultas

*Writing for Assessment*
Angela Goddard

*Transforming Texts*
Shaun O'Toole

# HOW TEXTS WORK

Adrian Beard

Routledge
Taylor & Francis Group

LONDON AND NEW YORK

First published 2003 by Routledge
11 New Fetter Lane, London EC4P 4EE

Simultaneously published in the USA and Canada
by Routledge
29 West 35th Street, New York, NY 10001

*Routledge is an imprint of the Taylor & Francis Group*

© 2003 Adrian Beard

Typeset in Galliard by Keystroke, Jacaranda Lodge, Wolverhampton
Printed and bound in Great Britain by TJ International Ltd, Padstow, Cornwall

*British Library Cataloguing in Publication Data*
A catalogue record for this book is available from the British Library

*Library of Congress Cataloging in Publication Data*
A catalog record for this book has been requested

ISBN 0–415–28634–4 (hbk)
ISBN 0–415–28635–2 (pbk)

# CONTENTS

# FIGURES

# PREFACE

## ASSESSMENT OBJECTIVES

The AS/A2 specifications in English are governed by assessment objectives (or AOs) which break down each of the subjects into component parts and skills. These assessment objectives have been used to create the different modules which together form a sort of jigsaw puzzle. Different objectives are highlighted in different modules, but at the end of AS and again at the end of A2 each of the objectives has been given a roughly equal weighting.

Particular assessment objectives that are focused on in this book are as follows.

---

### English Literature

**AO1**: in writing about literary texts, you must use appropriate terminology

**AO3**: you must show how writers' choices of form, structure and language shape meanings

**AO4**: you must provide independent opinions and judgements, informed by different interpretations of literary texts by other readers

**AO5**: you must look at contextual factors which affect the way texts are written, read and understood

---

### English Language and Literature

**AO1**: you must show knowledge and understanding of texts gained from the combined study of literary and non-literary texts

**AO2**: in responding to literary and non-literary texts, you must distinguish, describe and interpret variation in meaning and form

**AO3**: you must respond to and analyse texts, using literary and linguistic concepts and approaches

---

*continued*

**AO4**: you must show understanding of the ways contextual variation and choices of form, style and vocabulary shape the meanings of texts

**AO5**: you must consider the ways attitudes and values are created and conveyed in speech and writing

## English Language

**AO1**: in writing about texts, you must use appropriate terminology

**AO3**: you must show a systematic approach to analysing texts

**AO4**: you must show that you can understand, discuss and explore concepts and issues relating to language in use

**AO5**: you must analyse the ways contextual factors affect the way texts are written, read and understood

This book looks at six ways in which texts are often categorised. Each chapter begins by exploring some straightforward ideas that are raised by these terms, but then moves on to a more sophisticated model, which suggests that these labels of categorisation are open to further questions.

Each chapter contains a number of exercises. When the exercise introduces a new idea, there will usually be suggestions for answer immediately following. When the exercise checks to see if a point has been understood, suggestions for answer can be found at the back of the book.

Words defined in the Glossary are given in bold when used for the first time.

# ACKNOWLEDGEMENTS

The author would like to thank the following copyright holders:

Club 18–30, for permission to reproduce Extract from Club 18–30 Summer Brochure: Corfu/Tabukos Beach Club.

Denplan, for permission to reproduce their logo.

First Direct, for permission to reproduce a letter.

HarperCollins Publishers, for permission to reproduce the front cover of *Almost Paradise* © Susan Isaacs.

Ian Duhig, for permission to reproduce his poem, 'Another Poem About Old Photographs'.

National Union of Teachers, for permission to reproduce the NUT logo.

NatWest and TBWA, for permission to reproduce their student leaflet, *Your Guide to Managing Money.*

Nexus (Tyne and Wear Passenger Transport Executive), for permission to reproduce their advert.

Pret à Manger, for permission to reproduce a sandwich box.

Every effort has been made to obtain permission to reproduce copyright material. If any proper acknowledgement has not been made, or permission not received, we invite copyright holders to inform us of the oversight.

# REALITY AND REPRESENTATION    CHAPTER 1

This first chapter deals with ideas about what is real and what is a representation of reality. Such a question might sound very philosophical, but it is a crucial one for students of literature and language to answer.

The reason why this question is so important is that both language and literature appear to be very tangible entities, but are they? Literature offers us different worlds of action and character, and yet all literature is a world of words. And words themselves, language, are only labels for things: they are not the real things themselves. The word 'computer' is the name of the machine this book is being written on: it is not the machine itself.

## LANGUAGE AS AN ARBITRARY SYSTEM

The lack of any real connection between items of language and the objects named by language has often been pointed out. This is what is meant when people call language an **arbitrary system**.

The easiest way to start thinking about reality and representation is to focus on visual images. For example, think about an apple – any apple that you might see in a greengrocer's shop. The apple in the greengrocer's is real, but your mental image of it is a representation, an image created by a human agent. Any occurrence of an apple that is not the real thing, then, is a representation, whether it is an idea in an individual's memory, a line drawing, a photograph, a computer graphic or an oil painting.

## SIGNS AND SYMBOLISM

### Exercise 1

1. Write down what image you have in your mind when someone says the word 'apple'. For example:

- What colour is the fruit?
- Does the fruit have a stem and leaves attached, or not?
- Is the skin of the fruit shiny or dull?
- What angle are you viewing the fruit from — the top, the underside, the side?
- Is the apple whole, or has someone taken a bite out of it?
- Is the apple raw or cooked?
- Does the apple have a label of any kind on it?

2. Now look at these different images of apples in Figure 1.1. Explain what **connotations** there are: what qualities and ideas are you being encouraged to associate with each image?

*Figure 1.1* Apple symbols (a) NUT; (b) Denplan; (c) *Almost Paradise* and (d) Apple Computer

## Suggestions for Answer

When you think of an apple in the abstract – that is, without looking at a particular image – you probably have in mind a kind of idealised form. Despite seeing all the variations of apples around you, you probably think of a shiny red or green fruit, raw, perhaps with some stalk and leaves attached, pictured whole from the side rather than the top. This is the kind of image that is presented to us early on when we are learning to 'read' the objects around us. Psychologists call this idealised form a **prototype**. It represents the 'best' example of the object.

However, when you look at particular images such as these, it is a different story. The connotations of the images presented in the exercise are quite varied. The NUT (National Union of Teachers) loan advert uses an image of a bright, shiny apple to connote the idea of the 'teacher's pet' who reputedly brings the teacher an apple as a present. This 'present' has been individualised, presented as a specially selected item tailored to fit the person. It has a stamp of approval – the NUT logo – and it is freshly washed and looks tempting to eat.

The Denplan advert for dental healthcare payment plans also uses a whole, shiny apple, this time connoting the idea of health. Apples are seen as good for the teeth and for health in general: 'an apple a day keeps the doctor away'.

The other two images, for Apple Macintosh computers and for the novel, feature apples that have been tasted. The idea of the bitten apple has a long history all the way back to the Bible, where Eve was tempted in the Garden of Eden to eat the fruit from the tree of knowledge. In the biblical story, it was this act that led to the humans' expulsion from Paradise. The novel is referring to the biblical story in its title as well as in the image used.

The origin of the Apple Mac image is a bit more obscure. Of course, there is a well-known apple variety called the Macintosh; but one explanation of why the company chose a *bitten* apple is that of homage to Sir Alan Turing, a very influential figure in the development of computers who allegedly committed suicide by eating a cyanide-laced apple.

An important point to bear in mind from these notes is that there is no one single meaning for an image. You have seen that even one type of fruit does not have one uniform set of connotations. The different apple images can connote such different ideas as health and evil. Equally, your own reading of these images may well differ from that of other people, for a number of different reasons, including your culture and age.

The exercise you have just done should have made it clear that every time an object is represented, it appears in a specific way, according to the intentions and purposes of the author; but also that people bring their own experiences to how they view a visual image. Connotations are very much embedded in group culture, but, within that culture, individuals will have their own take on the associations that are linked to a particular word or image. It is sometimes useful to see the word representation as *re-presentation*: every presentation is a new occurrence, with its own set of circumstances.

At this point it is worth looking back and thinking about the very complex work that you did as a child, in order to understand the worlds of reality and representation. Your early picture books, those you 'read' before you could read words, offered you many experiences of representations. You learnt that these related to the real world, but that they were not real. When you saw a picture of an apple you didn't try to eat the page it was on. It was a conceptual feat on your part to see a relationship between a real apple and its pictorial representation, while at the same time perceiving difference.

The adult world offers many different types of representation. Images can appear in many different ways, from a photographic representation to a line drawing. How an image appears obviously affects the way we read it. But images can also have different kinds of relationships with what they stand for.

In **semiotics**, an image or other form of visual representation is called a **signifier**. So, in the previous exercise, the different apple images are signifiers. What each image represents is termed a **signified**. So ideas of happy classrooms and health are signifieds. The whole of the visual communication – signifiers and signifieds – is called **signs**. It's important to realise that how signs are read is not fixed, so when you are asked to analyse a sign, there is plenty to say about the different ways it could be interpreted.

A crucial concept in the interpretation of signs is that of **symbolism**. A symbol has no logical relationship with what it stands for, beyond that established by conventions of usage, and conventions of usage are all about culture. So, for example, even though apples may well be good for us, to have them stand for our overall health is symbolic. Of course, it is even more symbolic to propose a connection between apples and temptation, or apples and computers.

## Exercise 2

In Figure 1.2 are four images from computer graphics galleries. What do these images symbolise? To what extent are your associations logically connected with the image in each case?

*Figure 1.2* Images

Also consider how each image is represented. Would your response to the image differ if it appeared differently? For example, would you respond in the same way to a photograph of a real heart, or to a textile flag in the form of a pair of underpants?

We have been looking so far at images in isolation, but in reality, images rarely exist on their own. They form part of the way we read our environment, and they are integrated with verbal text to form **multimodal** messages.

## Exercise 3

Read the job advertisement in Figure 1.3, and answer the following questions:

- How does the visual image work? How does it appear? What are its associations?
- What connections are there between the image and the **hook** (the line in larger print that catches the reader's eye before they read the body of the text)?
- How do both these aspects connect with the **body copy** (the main part of the text)?
- What ideas are presented about the nature of the job being advertised, and about the nature of the candidate being sought?
- Describe the procedure you went through in order to make sense of this advert. For example, did you read the visual image first, then look at the verbal text? At what stage did you look at information about the advert's source (for example, the council's logo and address)?

There are some suggestions for answer on this exercise at the back of the book once you have completed this task.

# WE WANT YOU STIRRED BUT NEVER SHAKEN

## Executive Director c£45,000

Change is the single most demanding factor in local government today. Meeting its needs in a multi-disciplinary, politically and financially sensitive environment like ours might easily lead to a loss of nerve. Especially when issues like 'best value' are added to the mix. So joining the executive team responsible for driving through every change calls for a cool and confident manager with a steady hand. And a licence to thrill an attentive audience of some 80,000 taxpayers and 42 elected members. Which is why our Chief Executive and Deputy are keen to widen their partnership by introducing an ambitious, enthusiastic associate who can provide a strong sense of direction for specific line managers, taking direct responsibility for about half the council's £20 million budget. Determined and energetic, you'll have the management dexterity to motivate a diverse range of people with an equally diverse range of skills. You'll also be an accomplished troubleshooter whose aim is deadly when it comes to targeting solutions. It'll be your steer and your ability to influence others that will make you the agent of change this council needs to maintain its forward momentum. For an application form, please contact **EMRLGA, The Belvoir Suite, Council Offices, Melton Mowbray, Leicestershire LE13 0UL. Tel: 01664 502569 (24 hr answering service). Email: emrlga@emrlga.clara.net**

For an informal discussion contact Ursula Addyman or Janet Ward on 01664 502555.

**Closing date: 5th November 1999. Interview dates: 18th and 19th November 1999.**

*We encourage applications from men and women, from ethnic minorities and from people who perceive themselves to be disabled.*

*We operate a No Smoking Policy.*

*Committed to equal opportunities*     South Northamptonshire Council

*Figure 1.3* Job advert

To summarise what has been discussed so far:

- Words are labels for things, not the things themselves
- Words and images can carry certain connotations
- Images are often integrated into verbal texts
- Images and texts can have more than one meaning

## REPRESENTING TALK

So far, the focus in this chapter has been on visual communication, in the form of images and writing. But communication that occurs via sound can also be represented. Just as images and writing are subject to different interpretations, spoken language can also be represented and interpreted in many different ways.

## Exercise 4

Read through the transcript below, and try to make sense of the conversation that it represents. Make a list of the information that is lacking, therefore making it difficult for you to interpret the communication fully. When you have finished your list, order your points under the following headings:

- *Social context* (information about the speakers and their relationship)
- *Physical setting* (where they are)
- *Pragmatics* (shared information, assumptions made by speakers)
- *Prosodics* (aspects of sound)

Key to symbols:   (.) = normal pause
      [ ] = vocal effects
    **bold** = stressed syllables
     | = simultaneous speech
     A = Anne
     M = Mark

A:  hi
M:  hi
A:  I just been to feed the **cat**
M:  oh no
A:  he's been out in the **wild wind** (.) and **rain** (.) and he's really **cross** with me
M:  **is** he?
A:  I **played** with him for a bit (.) until he got **dry**
M:  what d'ya give him to **eat**?

```
A:  I gave him turkey
M:  hasn't he had that last tin of tuna yet?
A:  no I'm saving it up cos (.) we gotta leave him haven't we (.)
A:        | over the weekend
M:        | oh yeah
A:  thought I'd do a bit of              | bribery
M:                    | good thinking [laughter]
A:                              [laughter]
```

## Suggestions for Answer

### Social context

No information is given about who the speakers were – their age, their sex, where they live, what kind of relationship exists between them. In fact, M is Mark, A is Anne; they are partners who live together; they are in their forties, and they live in the north of England.

When the real conversation took place, these aspects of their lives were all relevant to how they communicated.

### Physical setting

There is no information about where the communication took place. In fact, Mark was at home when Anne arrived. He was busy in the kitchen when she walked in and greeted him, and as the conversation developed, Mark continued with preparing the dinner. Anne moved around as she talked, taking her coat off and getting a drink. Their conversation involved many examples of eye contact, facial expression, and bodily gesture: aspects that are often called **paralanguage**, or non-verbal communication. For example, when Anne talked about the wildness of the weather she dramatised her account by waving her arms around.

### Pragmatics

Some aspects of the language can only be fully understood when the participants' shared knowledge is taken into account. For example, it's unclear why A would feel it necessary to announce she had 'been' to feed the cat if the cat were in close proximity: she would be more likely to say 'I've just fed the cat', in that case. What we are not told is that Anne has been looking after a neighbour's cat, going into the neighbour's house especially to get the cat in each evening and feed it. Mark and Anne had spoken about this cat before, because it had been unsettled by being left by its owner. So when Mark replies to Anne by saying 'oh no', it's with a sympathetic wariness because he expects that the cat might have caused trouble.

### Prosodics

Although the transcript provides some information about the sound of the communication, that information is only sketchy. For example, although some stressed syllables are marked, there is no indication of pitch, intonation patterns, voice quality or accent. Laughter is represented at the end of the conversation, but there were many other vocal effects that were not included. For example, when Anne dramatised the wild weather and waved her arms around, she also elongated the word 'wild' and gave the word a whistling quality, to imitate the sound of the wind outside.

A paper-based representation can indicate aspects of speech, but there is no substitute for experiencing the sound. For example, simultaneous speech or laughter can be heard in tandem, but on paper it has to be registered by the reader as existing in separate spaces.

You should be aware as a result of doing the previous activity that when speech is transcribed, the researcher makes some decisions about how much detail to provide. These decisions have to be made because a transcript is a representation of the original text, not the conversation itself. The level of markings and other information given are likely to depend on the reason why the researcher wanted to 'translate' spoken language into a paper-based version in the first place.

## LITERARY CONVERSATION

## Exercise 5

The previous activity was about the nature of real speech and its representation in the form of a transcript. Now read through a literary representation of a conversation. How does it differ from the transcript you have just studied? Use the same four headings to help you organise your points:

- *Social context* (information about the speakers and their relationship)
- *Physical setting* (where they are)
- *Pragmatics* (shared information, assumptions made by speakers)
- *Prosodics* (aspects of sound)

> Donald is busy cooking when I get home. I go in to the boys. They are lying on the floor, heads close together, making an electric circuit on a board.
>
> 'It's going to be a burglar alarm for our room', says Joe. I watch Matt as he fits wire into the battery terminal. He doesn't look up or greet me. Joe may have forgotten the morning, but not Matt.
>
> 'I bought you something,' I say. Matt catches his bottom lip with his teeth, as if concentrating. 'I went into a little shop,' I go on. 'They had these screwdriver sets.' I take them out from behind my back. They are well-made, with smooth, heavy handles. There are eight in each set.

> 'Here you are. One each.' Matt's face flushes, very slightly. He hasn't expected a present. As I give him his, I slip two pound coins inside the plastic pack. 'And thank you for looking after Joe.'
> 'I didn't do anything. He's all right. He could've gone to school.'
> 'I couldn't, could I, Mum?'
> 'I don't think so. The way you looked this morning, Mrs Carmody would have sent you home. Dad'll look after you tomorrow, then it's the weekend.'
>
> H. Dunmore (1998, p. 79), *Your Blue-Eyed Boy*

## Suggestions for Answer

### Social context

Although there was information missing in the transcript of real speech you studied previously, the original conversation was self-sufficient and self-explanatory for the speakers involved. In novels, the speakers don't really exist, of course – they are creations in language. In order to make those creations work, the literary writer needs to fill in the kinds of details that we are aware of in our real social relationships. These details can be dispersed throughout a whole novel, so a single small extract will not necessarily be fully explanatory. However, in this extract, the reader is given quite a bit of information about family relationships, particularly the relationships between the mother and children, and between the two boys. But notice how much of that information is carried, not through the direct speech, but via the descriptions of non-verbal behaviour, such as 'Matt catches his bottom lip', and 'Matt's face flushes, very slightly'.

### Physical setting

These two texts show that what is expressed physically by real speakers has to be described in detail by the narrators of novels. As well as such aspects as facial expression and bodily gesture, characters' actions have to be outlined: for example, 'I take them out from behind my back'. In addition, details of the environment are needed: effort is put into setting Donald in the kitchen and the boys on the floor of the living room.

### Pragmatics

The shared knowledge that exists between real people enables them to operate in daily life without having to start from scratch at every moment. In novels, writers obviously imitate the ways real speakers interact, but there is a further complication, in that knowledge has to be shared with the reader as well as between the characters. For example, in this extract, the reader is reminded of an earlier event as an explanation of Matt's behaviour. Again, while in real life we simply behave, in novels behaviour has to be described and accounted for.

### Prosodics

While neither the transcript nor the literary extract convey the sound of conversation, the literary extract is very different in appearance from the transcript. The transcript is an attempt to be a scientific record, including specialist marks and codings devised by linguists; the literary extract is more concerned with giving the reader an impression of a certain kind of talk and uses only conventional punctuation to indicate the subtleties of speech. In the case of both the transcript and the literary text, readers bring their knowledge of the sound of speech to their reading. But in the literary extract, the effects that the reader responds to have been constructed by the writer. For example, the reader may well 'hear' the sound of a whining child to accompany the words: 'I couldn't, could I, Mum?'

One of the biggest differences between the real conversation and the constructed one is the completeness of the talk units in the literary extract. The literary writer is depicting family talk, which is hardly the most formal type of speech; and yet there is not a single overlap, interruption, incomplete or incoherent utterance, hesitation or change of tack. The idea that children, in particular, would do orderly turntaking, particularly if there had been some kind of emotional upset, is unlikely. The way we judge literary conversations, then, is not by comparing them with real ones, but by comparing them with other literary conversations we have read.

(For a more detailed exploration of the way talk is represented in literary texts, see the companion book in this series by A. Beard, *The Language of Literature*.)

All the differences we have been observing in the representation of talk relate to the purposes of the texts. In the end, people in real life have conversations for their own benefit, while literary conversations occur in order to develop a storyline. We will be thinking in more detail about the notions of purpose and audience in the chapters that follow and there will be further discussion of literary texts at the end of the book.

## Exercise 6

To explore further the ideas in this chapter, attempt the following research exercise:

- Tape record a casual conversation
- Decide on two aspects of speech you could investigate in your data. Then spend some time transcribing the conversation, using codings that are appropriate to the aspects of language you are interested in
- When you have done this, turn one of your transcripts into a text that would be suitable for use in a novel
- What changes have you made?
- What do the changes tell you about the different ways talk can be represented?

**SUMMARY**

This first chapter has looked at some aspects of reality and the representation of reality. In explaining representation, or re-presentation, it looked at visual signs and the various cultural connotations they can produce. In addition to discussing visual representation this chapter has also looked at representation of spoken language, including the representation of real speech in transcripts, and some of the ways in which literature represents talk.

# DEGREES OF PLANNING      CHAPTER 2

This chapter will look at notions of planning in texts, and will move from some basic work on the degrees to which texts are planned, to some more subtle notions of what lies behind the way texts are constructed and responded to. The word 'degrees' here is used to suggest the different amounts of planning that may have gone into a text.

The degrees to which texts are planned is a popular way of categorising texts, and clearly is connected to other areas of categorisation covered in this book, such as levels of formality and different types of purpose. Both written and spoken texts will be looked at here, including texts which are produced by individuals and texts which are produced by two or more people collaboratively.

## Exercise 1

1. To begin this chapter, think about the written texts that you have produced recently, including such items as notes (academic and personal), text messages, emails, and work out the amount of planning that you put into them. Have you, for instance, done any drafts first, made corrections, checked them over afterwards?
2. Now consider some spoken interactions you have had, such as phone calls, interviews with a tutor, conversations with friends. To what extent would you say these have been planned?

## Exercise 2

1. Place the following written texts in order, with the most planned first, the least planned last:

   a note to the milkman
   a school report
   a will
   an extract from a chatroom conversation
   a text message to a friend

2. When you have done this, do the same for the following spoken texts:

    a political speech to the nation
    two friends chatting face to face
    an exchange between two strangers waiting at a bus stop
    an exchange between a call centre worker and a member of the public

3. Finally, put all the texts together in one long list, again with the most planned first.

There are no right answers as such to these three tasks, but the suggestions which follow begin to open up some of the issues around notions of planning.

## Suggestions for Answer

In the written texts it is likely that the will came top of the list. This is a very formal document, which the 'owner' usually has produced for them by someone else – a solicitor. All the owner does is sign at the end. This document uses a form of words and presentation that is standard for all such documents, so it is highly structured and follows set patterns. The least planned will probably be the note to the milkman. There are two obvious reasons for this text being seen as relatively unplanned compared to the will. One is that it is composed quickly, the other that it is easily disposed of. The will, on the other hand, takes time to compose, or so the solicitor will suggest when charging for it, and is stored literally until we die.

In the spoken texts the political speech to the nation is likely to be top of most lists of planned texts. The least planned spoken texts are probably two friends chatting – the word chatting suggesting casual talk – and the strangers meeting at the bus stop.

When putting the two lists together, it should be clear that spoken and written texts can have equally high or low degrees of planning, depending on the context of their production. There is probably much the same degree of planning in the call centre exchange and the school report, even though one is spoken and one written.

## PLANNING AND WRITTEN TEXTS

This next section explores some issues concerning planning and written texts.

## Exercise 3

Read the following invented text which is a note written to a milkman. What features of this note make it completely 'wrong'? What might the note actually say?

20 Hotspur Road
Newcastle upon Tyne
NE6 3FG


Dear Milkman

Hi! How are you this morning? Not too cold out I hope. I thought I would make a nice cheese sauce tonight, so I think I will have an extra pint on top of my normal two. Make it the milk with the full cream top, will you, as it makes a nice creamy sauce.

By the way, this is my last day here for a while before I go to Ibiza on holiday with a couple of friends. Have you had your holiday yet?

Anyway, must rush. Hope to write to you again soon and thanks for the milk.

yours etc

Mike Robinson

## Suggestions for Answer

This letter has a number of features which suggest that it is in the wrong **register**. Both what it says and how it says it are inappropriate for the genre. This is a letter with formally constructed sentences, conventional modes of address at the beginning and end, a named signature, and so on. It is also inappropriate in its detail. Conventional notes do not ask after the milkman's well-being, say why the milk is needed or indicate where you are going on holiday and with whom.

A much more likely note, written by hand on a scrap of paper, probably in block letters would go something like:

ONE EXTRA FULL CREAM TODAY
THEN NO MILK FOR TWO WEEKS
THANKS

The fact that we recognise the first note to be in the wrong register and genre, though, does show that we have 'scripts' for certain situations; the very idea of genre suggests that writers and readers operate within known and pre-planned conventions. It would not take long to write the second note, and it is not the product of careful construction in the way that many written texts are, but it can be argued that it has certain elements in it which are the product of planning through our awareness of text conventions.

## Exercise 4

Whereas the note to the milkman was seen as relatively unplanned, the following extract from a will can be seen as highly planned. Make brief notes on some of the ways this can be seen in the text below, trying to consider ways in which the very general notion of a text being planned can be broken down into more precise and therefore useful categories of analysis.

---

**5. I GIVE** all my property whatsoever and wheresoever (not hereby or by any Codicil hereto otherwise specifically disposed of) to my Trustees **UPON TRUST**: –

**5.1** to sell the same with power to postpone such sale for so long as they shall in their absolute discretion think fit without being liable for loss

**5.2** to pay out of my ready money and out of the proceeds of such sale my debts and funeral and testamentary expenses and

5.3 to divide the balance remaining of my ready money and of such proceeds and all unsold property (hereinafter called my 'residuary estate') between my daughter **NAME** and my son **NAME** as shall survive me and if more than one equally absolutely

**6. I DECLARE** that if before my death (or after my death but before my trustees have given effect to the gift in question) any charitable or other body to which a gift is made in this my Will has changed its name or has amalgamated with or transferred all its assets to any other body then my trustees shall give effect to the gift as if it had been made (in the first case) to the body in its changed name or (in the second case) to the body which results from such amalgamation or to which the transfer has been made and **I DECLARE** that the receipt of the Administrator or other proper officer for the time being of the charitable body shall be sufficient discharge to my Trustees

**SIGNED** by

---

## Suggestions for Answer

In a general sense this makes hard reading. The legal profession would argue the need for watertight documents in the light of all the problems with contested wills. A more cynical view would be that this document denies access to a general audience and is therefore creating more work for lawyers in the future. Evidence of planning can be seen in aspects of visual presentation, vocabulary, and syntax, but it is at a **discourse** level, that this text shows a high degree of a certain sort of planning.

In terms of presentation the text has numbered sub-sections, use of capitals, use of bold, all of which are genre conventions of will making. Some of the vocabulary sounds quaintly archaic – 'whereof', 'hereunto' – and some highly technical – 'testamentary expenses', 'residuary estate'. The syntax is complex in that many of the sentences are very long, with many added comments in brackets. The whole of Section 6 is one sentence, and even that does not end with a full stop. Although there are times when relatively unplanned writing can be unwieldy in its syntax, this seems designed to be so. All of this suggests that wills in outline form are pre-planned; the highly technical and archaic language is not the product of an individual making an instant response.

Looking at the text as a whole, then, we can see plenty of aspects of a highly planned piece of writing. It has all the hallmarks of a text that is carefully designed to be precise in all its details – its purpose is to follow the client's instructions to the letter. When we think more broadly about the context here, though, it is unlikely that the individual solicitor who drew up the will needed to do a great deal of planning as such. There will be many aspects of this will which appear in all wills – many of the clauses will be available in a databank. The client uses the solicitor as a sort of guarantee of legal honesty rather than as someone who is going to make a unique document.

---

To summarise what has been discussed so far:

- We can talk in terms of degrees of planning
- Evidence for degrees of planning can be seen by the time taken to compose the text and how long it is meant to last
- Relatively unplanned texts often follow generic scripts
- Planned texts tend to have more complex levels of vocabulary and syntax

---

The next written text to be looked at is a hybrid in terms of being spoken or written: a chatroom 'conversation' involves two people exchanging 'chat' by typing responses to each other while their computers are connected on-line. The typing of text means that the exchange is written, but the almost simultaneous exchange of contributions is similar to spoken conversation.

## Exercise 5

Read carefully the chatroom log and answer the following questions:

1. What aspects of this exchange suggest unplanned spontaneity?
2. To what extent can elements of planned discourse be found here?

Suggestions for answer are given at the back of the book.

In the extract, Rose191 and THat talk about their yoga class which THat has attended but which Rose191 has missed. David is their yoga teacher.

| | |
|---|---|
| THat: | hello stranger |
| Rose191: | hi there |
| THat: | my legs are killing – yoga was dead hard |
| Rose191: | oh no you're going to be so much more advanced than me |
| THat: | we were jumping arpund all over the shop |
| Rose191: | did many sign up for the new level |
| THat: | no alot signed up for the same call but there was only about 6 of us there |
| Rose191: | was david a bit sad about that |
| THat: | i think we should keep it up over the easter break – i'll show u my new moves |
| Rose191: | ok |
| THat: | he didn't even take a reg |
| Rose191: | teaching is a funny old job |
| Rose191: | i'm knackered just finished an article |
| Rose191: | what r u up to? |
| THat: | it was really good though – he said i was ok to graduate to the next class – my obviously teachers pet when u are not there |
| Rose191: | huh! do you mind having a slow firned? |
| Rose191: | friend |
| THat: | just a work – a bit bored – we are moving offices next week so i should be sorting out my stuff |

## PLANNING AND SPOKEN TEXTS

The list of spoken texts at the beginning of this chapter concluded with 'an exchange between two strangers waiting at a bus stop'. Within the notion of degrees of planning, this form of talk would be seen as largely unplanned – after all, you have no idea that you are going to meet a stranger and you have no idea what the stranger is like as a person, beyond their appearance in front of you. It is, however, possible to imagine how the conversation might go – to role play this sort of talk is pretty easy. The ability to imagine a conversation like this says something about the nature of the conversation itself. So, for example, it might begin:

> A:  Morning, have you been waiting long?
> B:  Just missed one five minutes ago.

and it would certainly not begin:

> A:  Morning, have you read any Jane Austen novels?
> B   Yes, all the main ones.

The fact that we can predict within a certain range how such an exchange will go suggests that the way we talk is governed by our knowledge of what kind of communication is required in certain contexts. So, while we do not explicitly plan what we are going to say in case we meet a stranger, there is a form of hidden planning working within the context of the conversation.

## Exercise 6

(a)  Bearing in mind the work done so far on written texts, how does this spoken text show signs of being unplanned and spontaneous?
(b)  To what extent can this conversation also be seen to be working within certain expected conventions of this type of talk?

> Key to symbols: (.) = normal pause
> [ = simultaneous speech
> L = Lisa
> N = Natalie
>
> L:  like my new trainers
> N:  oh I thought they were new
> L:  yeah (1)
> N:  you bought Fila
> L:  what
> N:  Fila trainers
> L:  well they were cheap so (.) I got them for twenty-eight with my discount so [
> N:  [ yeah

*continued*

```
L:   I think the ones Sarah's got are [quite nice (1)
N:                                    [do you get discount on everything you buy
L:   apart from sales (.)
N:   do friends get it
L:   if you pay (2)
N:   oh
```

## Suggestions for Answer

Within the conversation itself, Lisa establishes the agenda in that she asks Natalie to comment on her new trainers. We have no means of knowing whether Lisa has planned to ask this question in advance of the meeting, but it is unlikely that she will have planned the exact form of words.

The agenda of the conversation moves on from the trainers when Natalie asks Lisa about discount. The pragmatics around this part of the exchange are quite complex. Although it is not stated, because both parties know it, we as readers of this text can work out that Lisa works in the shop where she bought the trainers. When Natalie asks a more general question about discount, though, we presume that she is making an oblique move towards asking if Lisa can get a discount for her too. To ask outright would risk possible embarrassment for both of them. Lisa's reply is not absolutely clear, and it is not clear either whether Natalie is sure what Lisa means. Her 'oh' may mean that she will return to the topic later.

Here, then, we can see some typical features of unplanned talk: pragmatic understanding; pauses for thought; repetition; overlapping speech. This is a long way from the type of language we saw used in the will: in terms of planning, the two texts are clearly very different. But, just as we saw that the will was not necessarily quite as carefully planned as might be suggested because of the likelihood that it has a pre-used format, so there are ways of looking at this spoken data which suggest that it is rather more planned than we might at first assume.

Although we have no access to any detailed knowledge about the relationship between the friends here, we may well know from our own friendships that conversations are characterised by certain features. So, for example, the way Natalie asks Lisa about discounts, and Lisa's reply, show each being considerate to the feelings of the other.

Even the pauses and overlaps, while not planned as such, are features of what most of us would expect from a friendly conversation. Although too much silence can be embarrassing, no silence at all can be unsettling too. What we do, in effect, is draw upon our experience of communication that we know works. This is a form of hidden planning, sometimes known as **scripts** in psychology. Scripts in this sense of the word can be defined as the behaviour appropriate to a particular situation that we have learned through previous experience.

In the previous exercise we saw that even spontaneous conversation has aspects of a learned script. The following exercise uses the idea of a script in a rather different sense of the word. This time there is an actual written script which one of the participants is using.

## Exercise 7

The transcript is a slightly edited version of a conversation between a worker in a call centre (W) who has cold-called a member of the public (P). Both are male. The transcript begins soon after the call starts.

Read the transcript carefully and show:

1.  How the worker (W) can be seen to be working from a planned script.
2.  How the receiver of the call (P) responds to this script.

Suggestions for answer are at the back of the book.

Key to symbols: (1) = 1 second pause
(.) = normal pause

W:  I'd like to ask you a few questions about the way (name of company) has dealt with the fault so far (1) would it be ok to speak to you now
P:  fine
W:  it just takes about 5 or 6 minutes ok
P:  pardon
W:  may I take your name please
P:  yep er (name supplied)
W:  (2) right in overall terms (1) how satisfied or dissatisfied were you with with the service
P:  oh it was no (.) no (.) no trouble at all it was fine
W:  right (.) so would you say you were extremely very or fairly satisfied
P:  um I'm I'm satisfied
W:  so again (1) is that extremely very or fairly satisfied
P:  extremely
W:  ok (1) and when you called the company to report this fault did you encounter the call steering system (1) this would be the recorded message which asked you to press buttons on your phone
P:  oh yes (.) yeah
W:  right (.) I'm gonna read out to you 3 statements about the call steering system
P:  right
W:  and for each one you tell me whether you agree or disagree (1) right (.) the range of options were sufficient for your needs

*continued*

```
P:   far more than sufficient but (.) yes
W:   it got you to the person that you had to speak to quickly and efficiently
P:   ultimately
W:   and the instructions were clear and easy to follow
P:   yep i'd agree with that
```
                                                                        Michael Alberici

## SUMMARY

This chapter has looked at written and spoken texts which have, to a greater or lesser degree, evidence of being planned. While looking at features of overt planning, it has also been shown that at a less obvious level we follow certain scripts when constructing texts. In written texts these scripts can involve working within the conventions of certain written genres. In spoken texts, the scripts are also generic in that speech events often follow certain patterns that we have learned through our past interactions with others.

# TEXTUAL PURPOSES

# CHAPTER 3

This chapter begins by looking at some of the main ways in which the purposes in texts are often categorised. It argues from the beginning that many texts have more than one purpose. This is illustrated first by looking at written examples, and then by spoken ones, with a special case made out for the representation of speech in fictional works such as plays. The chapter ends by looking at two texts where identifying the purposes requires some more sophisticated analysis.

## Exercise 1

1. Look at your school or college web-site, or search for any other similar site. What purposes would you say it is serving?
2. Think back to the last 'public' meeting you attended – which could be an assembly, a religious meeting, a work-based meeting, etc. What would you say were the main purposes of the speeches that were made?

## DIFFERENT PURPOSES

Whatever your personal experience of these texts, it should be clear to you that they potentially have more than one purpose. One way of categorising texts is by identifying their purposes, as they appear to you and other readers. Most students of English will be familiar with the notion of purpose from their work in GCSE and/or their own Original Writing at AS/A2. Purpose in these areas is usually defined in four broad areas, which are:

- Texts produced to *persuade*
- Texts produced to *instruct or advise*
- Texts produced to *entertain*
- Texts produced to *inform*

These areas, while being helpful in a general sense, do not, however, allow for some of the more sophisticated ways of looking at texts which are required when analysing and categorising texts, both written and spoken. There are three reasons why placing a text in one of these categories, and in one category only, can be problematic:

1.  The first problem comes in the fact that although many texts fall into the four categories above, not all do. A birthday card, for example, is a text in that it contains visual and written symbols. It could be that there is a verse in the card which could be defined as a text to entertain, but the whole card does not easily fall into any category. It clearly serves a social function, but it does not as such persuade, instruct, entertain or inform. Texts which make requests can also be seen potentially to fall outside these categories.
2.  Some texts may only have one purpose, but many others have more than one purpose. It is often possible to say that a text has a *primary* (most important) purpose, and one or more *secondary* (less important) purposes, but sometimes even these distinctions are not clear.
3.  When ascribing purpose to texts, it is sometimes forgotten that texts have a **context** – in other words, there are particular circumstances surrounding the way the text is produced and received. The purpose of the text as produced may not necessarily be the purpose of the text as received. What is intended as a polite request may be taken as a sinister threat.

## PURPOSE AND WRITTEN TEXTS

### Exercise 2

For each of the following written texts, identify its primary purpose and say whether it may possibly have secondary purposes:

> a note to the milkman
> a school report
> a slogan on a T shirt saying 'I have nothing to declare but my genius (Oscar Wilde)'
> a text message saying 'gd luck sweetie pie c u l8ter xx'
> a cheque
> a will
> a sponsor's logo on a replica football shirt
> an extract from a chatroom conversation

### Suggestions for Answer

There are no right answers to this task, but considering where to place these texts will have encouraged you to see some of the subtleties behind categorising texts by purpose. So, for example, the note to the milkman could be seen as informational ('Two pints today' means 'I need two pints'), or a request ('Please can I have two pints?').

School reports are almost certainly going to be informative, saying how the student is doing, advisory in that they will suggest ways to improve and persuasive in that they will offer incentives for improvement. Whereas once teachers were allowed to be entertaining in reports – usually at the expense of the student – this is now frowned upon.

To what extent the cheque can be categorised is also open to question; if you write a cheque you are perhaps informing, if you cash one you are perhaps requesting.

> To summarise what has been discussed so far:
>
> - Texts rarely have a single purpose
> - It is helpful to talk of a primary purpose and secondary purposes
> - Nearly all texts have some sort of informative function
> - The purpose of a text when produced may not be the same as the perceived purpose when it is received

The issue of purpose in written texts will now be explored by looking at one text in more detail.

## Exercise 3

The following text comes from a booklet on safety in the home. It deals with some basic issues concerning First Aid.

1. What would you say is the primary purpose of this text, and what language features have led you to this decision?
2. Is it possible to say that there are any other identifiable purposes in this text?

Some suggestions for answer follow after the text.

---

FIRST AID

If you are faced with an accident or emergency situation, what can you do to help?

**THESE ARE THE PRIORITIES**:

- **Keep calm, reassure the casualty.**
- **Assess the situation:**
  Is danger still present?
  Ask the casualty or any bystander what happened.

- **Make safe**:
  Make sure that there is no further danger to the casualty or yourself.

*continued*

---

- **Give Emergency Aid**:
  Don't do too much. If there is more than one
  casualty, treat in the following order:

  (1) Unconscious and not breathing;
  (2) Bleeding;
  (3) Fractures;
  (4) Other injuries

  Never give a casualty anything to eat, drink, or
  smoke.

- **Use bystanders to help you**:
  Get them to dial 999 emergency number.

## Suggestions for Answer

It should not be too difficult to work out that the primary purpose of this text
is to instruct/advise readers on how to behave during an emergency. The design
of the text is helped by bullet points and bold highlighting, in an attempt to make
sure that key issues are noticed. Many of the verbs are in the form of commands:
'keep calm', 'assess', 'make safe', 'give emergency aid', etc. The potential reader or
**narratee** of the text is addressed directly as 'you'. **Rhetorical questions** are used
twice. In the first example, the question 'what can you do to help?' is answered by
the section 'These are the priorities'. The second rhetorical question, though, is
left unanswered; 'Is danger still present' becomes another form of instruction – in
other words 'go and check there is no danger still present'.

Even with this text, though, it is possible to say that within the instructions lie
information. If you are told to deal with bleeding before fractures, then this informs
you by the clear implication that bleeding is a more serious injury than a fracture.
In the same way, we can say that giving a casualty a cigarette is not a good idea.

Informational aspects, then, are a clear feature of this text. Indeed, as we develop
more sophisticated ideas about the purposes that lie within and behind texts, it will
become clear that nearly all texts, whatever their most obvious purposes, are in some
ways informative.

## PURPOSE AND SPOKEN TEXTS

Spoken texts can have different degrees of formality and different levels of planning
(see Chapters 5 and 2 in this book on these topics). It is probably fair to say that
the more planned a piece of talk, and the more formal it is in its context, then the
easier it is to ascribe a purpose or purposes to such utterances. So, for example, if

a politician makes a speech to a public audience, he or she is likely to have a primary purpose of persuasion with this persuasion made more palatable, perhaps, by a certain amount of entertainment. On the other hand, a comedian, who will have at least some idea of a script in their head, will be aiming to entertain their audience, but at the same time may be trying to persuade them to consider a more serious point as well.

When we come to transcripts of spontaneous conversation, though, the picture is rather different. Transcripts of spontaneous conversation are an attempt to replicate 'real' talk. The word real is placed in inverted commas here, because in producing a transcript on paper, what has been produced is not real talk at all – too much has had to be omitted. So, for example, a transcript cannot show body language, facial gestures and all the other para-linguistic features that contribute to actual speech. Nor can a transcript show all the prosodic features, such as pitch and tone of voice which can affect the meaning of an utterance. When two or more people converse, they may have different agendas and take different things away from the talk. The purposes of 'real' talk are shifting and negotiated between the speakers as the talk progresses. If we attempt to ascribe purposes to a transcript of 'real' talk, we have to be aware that we are basing our judgements on our reading of a version of the talk that we have in front of us.

Although 'real' talk poses problems when identifying purpose(s), this is not the case in **represented talk**. Talk in such texts as novels, plays, adverts does have much more identifiable purposes. In addition to having an entertainment function, it is there to help create characters, develop the plot, create tension, show conflict, sell a product, etc. It can be analysed in different ways from 'real' talk, because it is talk that has been especially created for us as readers/viewers. One of the main ways in which represented talk is so different from 'real' talk is that its purposes are not only accessible to an audience, they are designed to be so. (For other aspects of represented talk, see Chapter 1 of this book and *The Language of Literature* by Adrian Beard in this series.)

It was stated earlier that the more planned a piece of talk, and the more formal it is in its context, then the easier it is likely to be to ascribe a purpose or purposes to such utterances. The nature of the audience for the talk is likely to be significant too. If the talk takes the form of a speech, where there is a single speaker and a listening audience, it is probable that the speaker will encode at least some of their purposes in what they say, even explicitly saying something like 'I am here today to warn you about the dangers of global warming.' The audience, although verbally passive, can still though shape how the talk progresses through their reactions – if they laugh, then the entertainment factor will rise, if they yawn it may need to! If they go as far as interrupting or heckling, then the speaker will have to adjust their original plans to accommodate this new turn of events.

## Exercise 4

The following speech was made by President George Bush on 11 September 2001, not long after news reached him of the terrorist attacks on the World Trade Center in New York and before news of the attack on the Pentagon in Washington. It was later made available on the Internet. At the time of the attacks the President was visiting a school in Florida, with the intention of making a speech about education.

Read the speech carefully and then identify what could be seen as the various purposes of the speech. Try to think beyond the four major labels, using the contexts within which the President was operating at the time to help you.

Ladies and gentlemen, this is a difficult moment for America. I, unfortunately, will be going back to Washington after my remarks. Secretary Rod Paige and the Lt Governor will take the podium and discuss education. I do want to thank the folks here at Booker Elementary School for their hospitality.

Today we've had a national tragedy. Two airplanes have crashed into the World Trade Center in an apparent terrorist attack on our country. I have spoken to the Vice President, to the Governor of New York, to the Director of the FBI, and have ordered that the full resources of the federal government go to help the victims and their families, and to conduct a full-scale investigation to hunt down and to find those folks who committed this act.

Terrorism against our nation will not stand.

And now if you would join me in a moment of silence. May God bless the victims, their families, and America.

Thank you very much.

## Suggestions for Answer

Although this speech would have had relatively little planning, it was made by a man who is used to making public speeches and who was surrounded by aides, so Bush would not have been as unprepared as most of the rest of us would have been. Although brief, the speech has a clear structure to it, and it shows that Bush is aware that he has at least two audiences. One is the audience in the school, the second is America and the whole world. His opening words address both those in front of him and those in front of their television sets. He also reassures his immediate audience that they have not been forgotten, and that their interests will be dealt with, although not by him.

George Bush, in making this speech, is both an individual man and a man in the role of the president, and he is talking both to the school audience and the national audience. The speech, therefore, is a mixture of the relatively intimate and the much more public. When he says, 'I, unfortunately, will be going back to Washington' the word 'unfortunately' is directed at the school audience – the nation as a whole would presumably want him to return. On the other hand 'this is a difficult moment for America' is much more directed at his wider audience. One word which surprised many people when they heard this speech was Bush's reference to the attackers as 'folks'. This makes much more sense, though, if we remember that he was addressing the school audience (whom he has also called 'folks') as well as the world audience.

Although the speech does provide some information, that is not really its main purpose. What George Bush is performing here is an act of social and political cohesion, made all the more subtle because of his double audience. He is attempting to give America reassurance that things are under control, defiance that such attacks will not be tolerated, promises that those who committed the attacks will be caught. Using a three part list, a favourite device in political speeches, he ends with a prayer, technically a request, but really a statement of solidarity. Clearly, then, there are elements of persuasion in this speech, but merely to label the speech as persuasive would be to over-simplify a very subtle text in terms of its overall purposes.

## Exercise 5

It was stated above that it is far more difficult to ascribe purposes to spontaneous conversation for two main reasons. One is that the written record of such a conversation is only partial in what it can show; it cannot show such things as facial expressions or tone of voice. The other is that we cannot assume that the participants either have a common purpose or that their individual purposes do not change as the conversation progresses.

To put this to the test, read the following transcript of a family conversation. To what extent is it possible to identify the purposes of each of the participants?

Key to symbols: (.) = normal pause
                [ = simultaneous speech
                F = father
                M = mother
                N = daughter (Nisha)
                P = son

P: dad, where you going (.) where you going
F: out
P: no really where you going
F: out
M: are you going to play badminton tonight
F: no you can't [come
N: [can I

*continued*

```
F:   it's for grown ups (1)
M:   ah, they can have a court (.) you can go and take them on another court
F:   yeah on a [separate court
P:            [I'm grown up aren't I
F:   no [separate they can go
N:      [ah go on
M:   if you wanna go then take them (.) why don't you two have a game
N:   mm
M:   why don't you two go (.) you don't have to play against Nisha (.) you can
     play against him
P:   I can beat [her easy
N:              [no you can't
```

## Suggestions for Answer

As expected, the absence of any para-linguistic and prosodic details makes this text difficult to evaluate in terms of purposes. We cannot know, for example, whether the father is determined to go out alone, or whether he is teasing his children and intends to take them along anyway. We can say with some confidence that the children are seeking information from their father, and that they are attempting to persuade him to take them out. But that is only part of their agenda. By the end of the extract they are arguing about who is the better player. The mother seems to want to persuade her husband to take the children, and to persuade the children to be co-operative, but this may be as much to do with keeping the peace as it is to achieving any ultimate goal.

What we have here then is a partial and shifting picture. While we can look at the various roles played by the participants, the way power seems to operate in this conversation, how turns are taken, and so on, it is not possible to take this text in its entirety and say that the conversation has a single purpose (it has a purpose within this book, that of exemplifying a point, but that is a different matter).

## Exercise 6

It was noted earlier that one of the main ways in which represented talk is so different from 'real' talk is that its purposes are not only accessible to an audience, they are designed to be so. Whereas the pragmatics of 'real' conversation allow the participants to understand what is going on, represented talk has to operate on two levels:

1. It has to show the characters' motives and purposes inside the text, within the created world of the story that is being told.
2. It has to serve the author's purposes outside the text by making sure an audience can follow the plot and develop ideas about the characters.

The following extract comes early on in the play *A Doll's House* by Henrik Ibsen (translated from the original Norwegian). Nora and Krogstad meet for the first time alone on stage. Read the extract carefully and then make notes on the following questions:

1. What can you work out about Nora and Krogstad's connection with each other? Why can you work this out relatively easily?
2. What are the possible motives of the characters within the play?
3. What could Ibsen's purposes be here?

Some suggestions for answer are given at the back of the book.

| | |
|---|---|
| KROGSTAD: | When your husband was ill, you came to see me to borrow twelve hundred dollars. |
| NORA: | I knew of nobody else. |
| KROGSTAD: | I promised to find you the money – |
| NORA: | And you did find it. |
| KROGSTAD: | I promised to find you the money on certain conditions. You were so much taken up at that time with your husband's illness, and so eager to have the means for your journey, that you probably did not give much thought to the details. Allow me to remind you of them. I promised to find you the amount in exchange for a note of hand which I drew up. |
| NORA: | Yes and I signed it. |
| KROGSTAD: | Quite right. But then I added a few lines, making your father security for the debt. Your father was to sign this. |
| NORA: | Was to – ? He did sign it! |
| KROGSTAD: | I had left the date blank. That is to say, your father was himself to date his signature. Do you remember this? |
| NORA: | Yes, I believe – |
| KROGSTAD: | Then I gave you the paper to send to your father, by post. Isn't that the case? |
| NORA: | Yes |
| KROGSTAD: | And of course you did so at once; for within five or six days you brought me back the document with your father's signature; and I handed you the money. |
| NORA: | Well? haven't I made my payments punctually? |
| KROGSTAD: | Usually – yes. |

## Exercise 7

The primary purpose of this chapter has been to show that texts often have more than one purpose. To complete the work on this topic, do the following exercise on Nexus.

Nexus (Tyne and Wear Passenger Transport Executive) owns and operates the Metro system throughout Tyne and Wear. They also own the Shields Ferry which operates between North Shields and South Shields. The name *Metro* is also given to a free newspaper which appears daily in the area and is distributed at various Metro stations.

Look carefully at Figure 3.1 and explore some of the purposes which can be seen to be at work within this text.

Suggestions for answer are given at the back of the book.

content supplied by

# NEXUS
### News and Information

www.nexus.org.uk

# National award for Metro campaign

**They say it pays to advertise and, for the marketing team at Metro operators Nexus, that old adage has certainly paid off.**

That's because the team scooped an award in a prestigious national advertising competition, the Travel Industry Advertising Awards.

The Nexus team, led by Head of Marketing Andy Bairstow and Marketing Manager David De Ivey, picked up a bronze award in the Display Classified Campaign category of the competition.

Their campaign beat off stiff competition from a clutch of leading, big-budget advertisers.

It capitalised on the high cost of fuel, the difficulties of travelling by car, and the value and ease of travel offered by the Metro.

The campaign made subtle changes to the names of fuel

> **The Nexus Metro entry was among those whose work employed imagination and simplicity"**
>
> **Will Awdry**
> **Judge chairman**

brands to highlight the advantages of Metro travel, and ran across local press and radio, in addition to appearing as a high profile poster campaign at Metro stations.

In conjunction with a ticket price promotion campaign unning at the time, the Taxaco campaign succeeded in raising additional revenue of £300,000.

What impressed the judges about the Nexus Metro campaign – aside from the fact that it was created by a relative unknown and on a tiny budget – was its simplicity and effectiveness.

Chairman of the judges, Will Awdry said "Those receiving prizes deserve real congratulations. As always, the true victors were the ads engaging enough to rent space in our brains for longer than it took to view them."

Andy Bairstow, said: "The award is fantastic news and we were delighted to receive it."

*THE SIX POSTERS USED IN THE AWARD-WINNING CAMPAIGN*

*Figure 3.1* Nexus advert

## SUMMARY

This chapter has explored some issues concerning the idea of identifying the purposes in texts, both written and spoken. It has argued that while broad categories are useful as starting points, a more sophisticated process of analysis will show texts can be seen to have more than one purpose. Through the examples used here, we have seen that key aspects to consider when categorising texts according to purpose include whether the text is spoken or written, who has produced the text and in what contexts and whether it has a single audience or a multiple audience.

# PUBLIC AND PRIVATE CONTEXTS

This chapter will focus on the way texts differ in their contexts, particularly in how publicly or privately they work.

Thinking about publicity and privacy is important because these aspects are strongly connected with how texts address their audiences. An email you write to an individual friend is likely to adopt a very different style from the one you circulate to a largely unknown group of work colleagues. A good textual analysis will pick out what some of those stylistic differences are; an excellent analysis will link those differences with some speculation on why such differences occur. How writers imagine their texts will be read and heard – by whom, in what setting, over what timescale – will strongly shape how those writers use language in the first place.

## TEXTS AND AUDIENCES

This book has already provided you with a number of texts that differ in how public or private their contexts originally were. Of course, now that these texts are in this textbook, they are all public, but many did not start life in that way. For a text to move from a private to a public context, the writers/speakers have to agree: this is what is known as copyright permission. Everyone whose text has featured in this book has given their permission for their words to be made public, from the chatroom participants to the call-centre operator. In fact, permission is required even for those texts that are already in the public domain, for example, permission has to be obtained to reproduce literary texts. In that case, it is not so much a shift from private to public as a shift between different sorts of public contexts. Copyright law says that each context in which a text appears is, in essence, a new appearance; and writers and their publishers retain control over whether each new context is an acceptable one.

## Exercise 1

Here is a list of some of the texts that have appeared in this book so far. Page references are given so that you can refresh your memory about the nature of each text. Which of these would you say belonged to the public sphere, and which to the private sphere, in their original appearance?

Spend a few minutes assigning each text either to a 'private' or 'public' context, then read the discussion that follows.

| Text | Page |
|------|------|
| *Advertisements* | |
| South Northamptonshire Council | 7 |
| Nexus | 35 |
| | |
| *Face-to-face conversations* | |
| Anne and Mark | 8–9 |
| Lisa and Natalie | 21–2 |
| Family | 31–2 |
| | |
| *Literary extracts* | |
| Novel *Your Blue-Eyed Boy* | 10–11 |
| Play *The Doll's House* | 33 |
| | |
| Will | 18 |
| Call-centre phone call | 23–4 |
| First aid booklet | 27–8 |
| Political speech | 30 |

On the face of it, this list is quite easy to divide. Advertisements, literary texts, advice booklets and political speeches all exist in the public domain because, in theory, any member of the general public has access to them. They are not aimed at named individuals but at large numbers of anonymous readers or listeners.

On the other hand, the face-to-face conversations, the will, and the call-centre phone call all involve particular individuals having interactions that were never intended to be widely published. So an initial assigning of the texts may look like this:

| *Public* | *Private* |
|----------|-----------|
| Advertisements | Conversations in the home |
| Literary texts | Wills |
| Booklets | Phone calls |
| Speeches | |

Thinking in more detail about the texts on the list raises some more complex differences, however. For example, although the will and the call-centre phone call

all involve specific, private individuals, those texts can all become publicly available in particular ways. A will is private while an individual is alive, but when they die it becomes a public statement of their intentions. Call-centre phone calls are often recorded for training purposes, so could well form the basis of an in-house company training session where the interaction is broadcast to many listeners.

While supposedly private texts can move into the public sphere, texts aimed at the wider public are rarely written without a sense of private individuals. For example, look back at the South Northamptonshire job advertisement, which uses a direct address – 'you' – in its hookline. Recall what was said about the narratee for that text: what kind of idealised reader is set up by the language used in the advert? This advert is a good example of a common trend in contemporary advertising and promotional material, which is to humanise and personalise a public text by giving it a sense of personal reference. This book itself addresses 'you' as a single reader, when in fact it is produced for many readers. The material that follows will explore this idea further.

## Exercise 2

Look at Figures 4.1 and 4.2, which are both forms of advertising by large companies. Figure 4.1 is a piece of promotional mail which was addressed personally to a real individual. The names and addresses of real people are available to companies via a variety of routes which allow individually addressed pieces of communication, including electronic versions of letters and circulars. Figure 4.2 is from the packaging of a box of sushi sold by a sandwich shop.

Both the texts involve aspects of personalised reference, despite the fact that they are both forms of public, corporate address.

1. Explain how the personal references work in each text, and comment on the nature of the language use into which those references are integrated.
2. Why is it a useful strategy for these companies to use language in the ways you have identified?

Note: there are no answers provided for this exercise.

First Direct
40 Wakefield Road
Leeds
LS98 1FD

# first direct ◁X▷
*Member* HSBC *Group*

**0800 24 24 24**
**firstdirect**.com

February 2001

Dear Ms Smith

## Why would a bank pay you money?

Remember that mailing we sent you recently? The one that talked about why First Direct banking is so different. And offered you £15 when you opened an account? You've got it somewhere. But hey, life's too short to worry about changing your bank. Or is it?

## Banking is boring

That's why we went to make banking as simple and convenient as possible. Forget trekking to a branch and standing in a queue, just pick up the phone or click on our website, 24 hours a day, 365 days a year. You can pay a bill on Christmas Day, order a statement at midnight or discuss a loan at two in the morning with a real (and very helpful) person.

## Virtually perfect

With us, you can do your banking from anywhere you can lay your hands on a phone or a computer. From your desk or armchair, in bed, in the bath or on the beach. And when you need cash you won't have to go far our of your way either. You can withdraw up to £500 free of charge from us, from over 31,000 cash machines in the UK, including HSBC Bank and LINK network cash machines. Sounds ideal? It is. For further information please see the enclosed brochure.

## Free banking even when you're in the red

Many banks will tell you their services are free, but if you go overdrawn by as little as £10 you are often hit by unexpected charges. When you join First Direct you'll automatically be given a fee free overdraft of £250 which comes in especially handy towards the end of the month.

## Plus £15 credit before you start

If you open a First Direct current account before 31 May 2001, we'll add £15 to your opening balance. Now that really is different.

## Honestly, would you recommend your bank to a friend?

94% of our customers have recommended First Direct to their friends and relatives and 86% of our customers said they were 'extremely' or 'very' satisfied with the service we give them.

**It's a doddle**

Changing your bank account is not the hassle it used to be. Transferring your account is straightforward and simpler than you might think. For now, all you have to do is make sure you complete the enclosed application form and return it to us. (By 31 May 2001 if you'd like the sound of £15 paid into your account.)

If there's anything else you'd like to know, call us free any time on **0800 24 24 24**, about anything at all. If you have already been in touch, then we're sorry to have troubled you again.

I look forward to welcoming you.

Your sincerely

David Mead
Customer Services Director

PS Don't forget, when you open an account with us and have a credit balance before 31 May 2001, we'll pop £15 into your account.

*Figure 4.1* First Direct letter

*Figure 4.2* PRET packaging

Exercise 2 should have helped you to realise that, just because a text is in the public domain and originates from a large business or institution, it doesn't have to use formal and distant types of language. Texts can therefore be public in the sense of widely available, but still sound personalised in the way private forms of communication do.

The same comments could be made about literary texts. Literary authors of course want their readers to feel as if they are being individually addressed, even though we as readers know – and writers hope – that we are one of many thousands or even millions of individuals who will read the book. Literary writers sometimes use personal forms of communication – such as letters, diary entries or intimate emails – as the vehicles for their narrators' or characters' communication, and, of course, no literary dialogue would work at all without giving us the sense that we are eavesdropping on characters in their personal interactions.

Perhaps one of the oddest things we sometimes do as readers of literary texts is to take our book to the author for signing, as if that signature made our book different from the copies resting in the hands of the others waiting in the bookshop queue. However, it's important to realise that conventions and social practices change over time, so perhaps our behaviour in this respect is the result of the growth of the book industry as a mass market; because we know we are buying mass-produced objects, having a personal marker is all the more important. After all, as children we love writing 'this book belongs to _____'.

The idea of books as objects experienced in isolation is another relatively recent development, according to Baron (2000), who claims that we only have the phrase 'silent reading' to describe that practice because previously books were usually read aloud in communal spaces. Although this practice is still used in many primary classrooms, it is not seen as appropriate adult behaviour in contemporary culture. However, some analysts claim that the developments we are witnessing in new forms of electronic communication are likely to re-define the way we use texts, including how private or public certain texts (and their associated spaces) are thought to be.

## PUBLIC/PRIVATE COMMUNICATION AUDIT

In what follows, you will be thinking about your own practices and deciding what the public/private boundary means to you in your own language use. As a result of doing this work on your own practices, you will be in a better position to analyse the texts produced by others.

## Exercise 3

Answering the questions below will help you to build a picture of how you define and use certain types of text.

If you have not experienced the scenario in question yourself, the next best thing will be to answer on the basis of what you have witnessed in the behaviour of others.

## Telephone calls

1. In your opinion, mobile phone calls are:

    (a) private interactions
    (b public interactions
    (c) Either, depending on the circumstances

2. Now answer these questions:

    (a) If you believe that mobile calls are private, what steps do you take in your own behaviour to ensure that they remain so?
    (b) If you believe that mobile calls are public interactions, what in your own behaviour of taking and making calls shows that you believe this?
    (c) If you believe that mobile calls can vary in how private or public they are, explain what triggers this variation. For example, is it the identity of the caller, the topic of conversation, the setting you are in? How do you then adapt your behaviour accordingly?

3. Why, in your opinion, is there a growing demand for 'silent carriages' on trains, where mobile phone use is not allowed? In such carriages, should text messaging be banned as well as phone calls?
4. What do you think when you overhear other people's phone calls?
5. Has hearing others' phone calls changed your phone behaviour in any way?
6. Have you ever got into an argument or difficulty as a result of mobile phone use?
7. Do you think the development of mobile phones is having an effect on the use of traditional, land-line phones? How do the two types of phone call differ, in your experience?

## Text messaging

1. According to a recent estimate (BT, as reported in the *Independent*, 27 February 2002), 12 million text messages are sent in the UK every day. Why is this form of communication so popular, in your opinion?
2. If you send a text message, do you assume that the person you're sending it to will be the only reader, or are you aware that others might read it? How do your perceptions shape the way you communicate?
3. Have you ever read a text message that was intended for someone else? If so, how did you feel? Did you own up?
4. Have you ever sent a text message to the wrong person by accident? If so, what was the result?
5. List some of your most frequently used icons and other abbreviations. Do you reserve any of these for specific people, and for them alone?

### Computer-based communication

1. Do you share email accounts with anyone, or have easy access to another person's account? If so, have you ever read emails addressed to someone else, either accidentally or on purpose? If so, how did you explain that you had done this? (Most email programmes indicate by a change of icon that an email has been read.)
2. Has someone else ever read emails addressed to you? If so, how did it feel? Did you tackle the person and, if so, how?
3. Have you ever forwarded an email to the wrong person and caused yourself some embarrassment? Explain what the results of your mistake were.
4. When you get an email that has been sent to several people at once, do you check out who else is on the list, in order to see who you're being ranked with? Are you ever annoyed by what you find?
5. Have you ever sent an email to a particular person, then found that they have forwarded it to people you would have addressed differently if you'd been warned it was going further?
6. If you start an email which is then added to by someone else – perhaps they interleave their comments with yours, breaking up your original text – do you then feel that it stops being 'yours' and becomes something more collaboratively owned?
7. If you use chatrooms or instant message systems, do you ever save the chatlogs from the screen? If so, do you tell anyone you are chatting to that you are going to do this?
8. Have you ever 'stolen' icons or text from a website? Is it OK to do this, in your opinion? Are web-sites public texts that should be shared by all, or products of individual effort that should belong to their creators?

## Exercise 4

Many of the issues raised in Exercise 3 could form the basis for a language investigation. Additionally you could collect some material along the following lines, in order to do some investigative work on language use in public/private contexts:

- Forms of corporate advertising that use personalised references
- Notes on mobile phone use in public spaces
- Text message formulas and icons
- Examples of computer-based communication (e.g. emails, webpages, chatlogs) that raise interesting questions for you about public and private spaces.

**SUMMARY**

This chapter has explored some issues concerning the notion that texts inhabit public or private spheres. It has shown that in many ways this can be a crude distinction and that more sophisticated analysis shows texts can be widely available yet still seem personalised. Texts which seem essentially private can move into the public sphere, while texts aimed at a wider public are often written with a sense of being read by private individuals: texts can be widely available but still sound as if they are addressing *you*, the individual.

# FORMALITY AND INFORMALITY

This chapter will look at some ideas concerning formality and informality in written and spoken texts. It is probably easier to recognise formality and informality than to define or describe the concepts. In Figure 5.1 most people would be able to recognise that phrases such as 'chit chat', 'know the score', 'get the message' and 'stay in the know' are informal expressions that are used regularly in everyday discourse but not in formal contexts. Job interviewers are unlikely to say to their interviewee, 'We're ready for you now, so please come in for a chit chat.'

*Figure 5.1* Orange Just Talk advert

## THE IDEA OF FORM

The terms 'formality' and 'formal' are associated with the idea of rules and conventions, of doing the acceptable and respectable thing, of following established procedures or 'form'. You can see these ideas in the phrases below:

> please wear formal dress
> he didn't have a formal education
> they made a formal complaint
> it was a formal dinner party

'Form' can also mean 'shape':

> he saw a ghostly form on the stairs
> she admired his slender form
> her ideas took on a literary form
> he's in impressive form

These two groups of meanings are connected in language study, in that there is a perceived connection between rules of behaviour and the shape of language use: obeying established procedures of 'form' means using the right 'language forms'. Using the right language forms doesn't necessarily suggest we see them as meaningful, however: if someone says to you, 'It's just a formality', they are suggesting that you need to use the right words but you don't have to believe in them.

## RITUAL AND REPERTOIRE

Using the right language forms in a particular context doesn't necessarily mean using language that is peculiar or that occurs nowhere else. For example, when people say 'I do' in a marriage ceremony, they are not using unusual language. It is rather that using those words in that context means something special when the two aspects – language and situation – occur together. In considering formality of language use, then, the first question to think about is the context of its occurrence.

An early attempt to look at language as a form of behaviour in particular contexts was that of Speech Act Theory, which saw language as a way of doing things: committing oneself to promises, uttering threats, swearing oaths, making announcements.

## Exercise 1

1. Make a list of rituals or ceremonies that have particular uses of language attached to them. If you know more than one language, include examples from your other language(s).
2. Is there anything exclusive about the language used? (Does the language used only ever occur in that context, or does it occur elsewhere?)
3. In each case, what is the language *doing*?

Rituals and ceremonies are often easy to spot in any culture because they have certain types of dress and behaviour associated with them, of which language forms an important part. However, there are many less well-defined situations where a certain type of language is expected. This is as true of informal language use as it is of the formal kind. For example, using Standard English in a context where street slang is expected is as problematic as the other way around. So, although the term 'informal' might suggest an abandonment of rules and regulations, in reality, informal contexts are still quite rule-bound. It is probably better to think of the term 'informal' as denoting unofficial/familiar contexts and types of language use, rather than as language use without rules and conventions.

## Exercise 2

Everyone has a **repertoire** of different styles of language which they use for different purposes and audiences in a variety of contexts. If you are bilingual or multilingual, it may well be the case that you use a whole different language in some situations. If you are monolingual, you may vary in how much you use dialectal forms of language.

1. Make a list of three or more different situations where you vary your language use.
2. When you have finished, group the situations under the headings of 'more formal' and 'less formal'. For each group, try to identify some aspects of language which vary in your own repertoire of styles.

The English lexical system contains a wide range of **synonyms** that vary in formality. One way to tap into this system quickly is to think about the terms available to speakers to express **taboo** subjects, such as bodily functions, sex, and death. For example, which terms would you use in formal and informal settings to say you were going to visit the toilet? (Note that a choice of term had to be made for the previous sentence: the expression 'visit the toilet' is by no means neutral in its connotations.)

The reason why taboo areas are useful to consider is that taboo-related terms often express extremes of polite avoidance (**euphemism**) and crude directness (**dysphemism**). These extremes often correspond with formal and informal usage and reflect the fact that with respect to sensitive topics, there is little middle ground of relaxed and **unmarked** usage.

Beyond the initial thinking you have been doing on taboo terms, you may find it difficult to assess your own vocabulary in any real detail. The activities suggested below are therefore designed to give you some further practical examples and get you thinking further.

## THESAURUS AND ETYMOLOGY WORK

A thesaurus is a synonym dictionary where you can find lists of lexical variants. This is a good place to start exploring how different English terms may be associated with formal or informal contexts.

An **etymological** dictionary will give you information about the origins of words. This may be useful to know because many of our more formal English terms derive from French and Latin as opposed to Anglo-Saxon or Scandinavian sources. The fact that French and Latin-based words are associated with more formal styles is the result of the way those words came into the language historically via the usage of the more educated, powerful groups in English culture. Thesauri and etymological dictionaries can be accessed on-line: for example, go to http://www.yourdictionary.com

## Exercise 3

Look up six different words in a thesaurus. Here are two possible starters:

> work
> food

List some of the variants offered for each word, then arrange the terms according to how formal or informal they seem. Then look up each word in an etymological source.

Here is a brief example, based on a random choice of the synonyms of the verb 'to end':

> terminate
> conclude
> finish
> close
> stop

In this case, 'terminate' and 'conclude' seem more formal than the other three. This isn't just because they are longer words in themselves, although word length can be a factor because longer English words are often the French or Latin based ones. These terms are in fact Latin based: terminate is from *terminare*, 'to limit'; conclude is from *con*, 'completely', and *claudere*, 'to shut'.

A speaker's sense of the relative formality of a word will be the result of how they have experienced it in usage. For example, it seems that fairly significant or official things are terminated and concluded – pregnancies, employment contracts, examinations. On the other hand, fairly everyday things seem to finish, close or stop – TV programmes, doors, rain.

To summarise what has been discussed so far:

- The terms formlity/formal are linked to ideas of rules and conventions
- In language study rules and conventions are linked to the shape of language used
- Informal texts are still in many ways bound by rules
- Our sense of formality in language comes from our experience of language use

So far, all we have is an individual's intuitions of language use. Of course, other speakers can always be canvassed on their experiences, to arrive at more of a group judgement. But there are now also some very useful electronic resources that enable linguists to see how particular words are used in context: language corpora of many millions of words can be stored and searched to see what environment a chosen word tends to appear in. Although we are all benefiting in general from this method of analysis (called 'corpus analysis') because it now forms the basis for modern dictionary descriptions, there are ways that A Level students of English can access language corpora for specific searches.

## Exercise 4

Choose one of the words from the lists you compiled, and search for it on the website of the British National Corpus (a collection of many millions of words from both spoken and written sources) at the following address: http://info.ox.ac.uk/bnc

When you are on the site, you will need to go to the BNC On-line Service, and choose to do a 'Simple Search'. This will show you your chosen word embedded in a series of randomly chosen sentences, so you will be able to see the ways in which your word tends to be used. Because this is a free service, you will only be given fifty lines, but this will be enough for you to see the potential of this type of analysis.

Space prevents extensive illustration here, but below are the first few lines from simple searches done on 'terminate' and 'stop', respectively. The codings indicate which texts the extracts are from. See how far the examples back up the descriptions of these terms above.

**terminate**

A01 272 The length of the covenant will have been specified in the Deed, and it will terminate when the last specified annual payment has been made.

A1V 712 With the political dust not yet settled from a controversial abortion ruling in July, the nine Supreme Court justices must rule in the next nine months on three other attempts by US states to regulate abortion as well as the right of parents to terminate the life of a brain-dead daughter.

A6A 2082 Like any legal agreement, if there is a material breach by either party there should be a right for the injured party to terminate the contract.

AS1 979 The connections are sealed joints and only the Electricity Board may make these joints and provide the two service wires to each house, where they terminate in a sealed, fused container.

ASK 1730 It is as follows: that the decision to turn off a ventilator is, in fact, a decision to terminate the life of a patient or to remove from a patient the last thread by which he held on to life.

B08 1193 Nor is it necessarily fatal if you give notice to terminate your contract and work that notice out, rather than walking out on the spot.

B3K 194 The train will normally terminate here.

**stop**

A0J 1596 Stop smoking

CEJ 750 It should be noted, however, that the symbolism does not stop at this point.

CH2 13110 Pint glasses must be an eighth of an inch taller from April 1994 to stop publicans serving short measures.

CH6 1652 Devoted housekeeper Annie Bowman was crushed to death as she tried to stop a thief stealing her boss's JCB digger.

EF1 2774 And her mother was too weak to stop his drinking.

F9X 631 Ace caught it, almost pulled Defries from her perch, released it, and rolled to a stop a few metres further down the slope.

H7R 1292 (Alternatively the 'count = O' signal can stop the clock directly.)

H8L 1778 In the small triangle of dust the tip of a finger had written plainly GB, and jabbed a plump round full stop after the letters.

So far, the idea of formality has been linked to differences in how official or everyday the contexts of usage were. There are some further aspects that may also have a bearing on an individual's perception of lexical usage in a text.

Perceptions of formality are often about words seeming unfamiliar because they are not in the experience of an individual. Sometimes that is not so much about official usage as about language use in a restricted or specialist area, for example, scientific language. This is known as a **semantic field**.

It may also be the case that specialist groups retain forms of language that have died out in general usage. This is true, for example, of the legal profession, where the emphasis has been on terms and concepts retaining a fixed meaning over long periods of time. When terms have dropped out of general usage, they are known as **archaisms**.

## Exercise 5

Look again at the will (known in its full title as a Last Will and Testament) that you saw first in Chapter 2. If formality is about official types of language use, this type of text would probably be seen as a good example.

---

**5. I GIVE** all my property whatsoever and wheresoever (not hereby or by any Codicil hereto otherwise specifically disposed of) to my Trustees **UPON TRUST**: –

**5.1** to sell the same with power to postpone such sale for so long as they shall in their absolute discretion think fit without being liable for loss

**5.2** to pay out of my ready money and out of the proceeds of such sale my debts and funeral and testamentary expenses and

**5.3** to divide the balance remaining of my ready money and of such proceeds and all unsold property (hereinafter called my 'residuary estate') between my daughter **NAME** and my son **NAME** as shall survive me and if more than one equally absolutely

**6. I DECLARE** that if before my death (or after my death but before my trustees have given effect to the gift in question) any charitable or other body to which a gift is made in this my Will has changed its name or has amalgamated with or transferred all its assets to any other body then my trustees shall give effect to the gift as if it had been made (in the first case) to the body in its changed name or (in the second case) to the body which results from such amalgamation or to which the transfer has been made and **I DECLARE** that the receipt of the Administrator or other proper officer for the time being of the charitable body shall be sufficient discharge to my Trustees

**SIGNED** by

---

Which items of language would you pick out as illustrating formality? Include consideration of semantic fields and archaic usage. So far, the focus has been on **lexis**, but you should also consider grammatical and **graphological** aspects of the text.

## Suggestions for Answer

There are many lexical items in the text that all belong to the general semantic field of money and goods: for example, 'sale', 'proceeds', 'ready money', 'property'. However, some terms in this field are legal specialisms, that is, they occur only in legal contexts and have a restricted meaning, thus appearing formal to the uninitiated. An example is the term 'Trustees', which refers to people who will be 'trusted' to manage the financial affairs of an individual or company.

There are many terms in the text that have connotations of official usage, for example, 'dispose', 'discretion', 'testamentary expenses', 'residuary estate', 'charitable body', 'amalgamation', 'sufficient discharge'. While all of these words and phrases are part of the English language, they are unlikely to occur very often in the everyday interactions that we engage in, particularly of the spoken type. All of them have less formal equivalents, for example, to 'dispose' is to 'get rid of', 'residuary estate' is 'what's left over'. The fact that legal officials use 'dispose' and 'residuary estate' is to do with the fact that legal documents follow rules and conventions that have remained unchanged for many years. These terms have acquired a specific meaning in legal usage and to change the terms would be to open up the possibility of constant challenges to meaning.

An additional consideration (see the earlier suggestions for answer on this text in Chapter 2, page 19) is whether we would be happy to pay for someone to write our will using phrases such as 'what's left over', not because this phrase is unclear, but because we see specialist language as the product of experts and as having official legitimacy. If we pay for something, we expect it to be better than what we could do ourselves.

Some grammatical aspects of formality are also based on long-standing usage, and triggered by the need to close any possible loopholes (and/or retain a sense of specialism). For example, in saying 'I give all my property *whatsoever* and *wheresoever*', and in saying '*absolute* discretion', the **modifiers** in italic endorse the fact that there are no exceptions allowed. Because the idea of not allowing exceptions to meaning is not one that is at the forefront of our minds in everyday contexts, such hammering home of points would be seen as repetitive and unnecessarily precise in less formal interactions. For example, if you said to a friend 'I will meet you for coffee or a beverage of equivalent value in the bakery in the High Street at precisely 11 a.m. and in that establishment and absolutely no other', they would either think you had gone mad or were using elevated and over-precise language for humour.

Nowadays, although 'whatsoever' can be heard in less formal contexts, the terms 'wheresoever', 'hereby' and 'hereto' are archaic. As with similarly archaic terms seen in other legal documents – such as 'whereupon', 'howsoever' and 'heretofore' – these items often mark out areas of **deictic reference**. In other words, they define the scope of the statement being made, by pointing to aspects of time and space. Such pointers are important in legal documents because they express the 'where, when and how' of promised actions.

Finally, the actions promised by the will are expressed via unusual graphology. Look at the unconventional capitalisation on 'I GIVE' and 'I DECLARE' for example.

## Exercise 6

The language of chatrooms is often considered to be an informal type of written language (Werry, 1996).

Here is the chatroom dialogue you considered in Chapter 2. After working on the language of the will, you now have a certain type of formal language in your mind. How does the chatroom compare with the will, in terms of formality? Again, go beyond vocabulary to consider other aspects of language use, such as non-standard usage and grammar.

Suggestions for answer are given at the back of the book.

| | |
|---|---|
| THat: | hello stranger |
| Rose191: | hi there |
| THat: | my legs are killing – yoga was dead hard |
| Rose191: | oh no you're going to be so much more advanced than me |
| THat: | we were jumping arpund all over the shop |
| Rose191: | did many sign up for the new level |
| THat: | no alot signed up for the same call but there was only about 6 of us there |
| Rose191: | was david a bit sad about that |
| THat: | i think we should keep it up over the easter break – i'll show u my new moves |
| Rose191: | ok |
| THat: | he didn't even take a reg |
| Rose191: | teaching is a funny old job |
| Rose191: | i'm knackered just finished an article |
| Rose191: | what r u up to? |
| THat: | it was really good though – he said i was ok to graduate to the next class – my obviously teachers pet when u are not there |
| Rose191: | huh! do you mind having a slow firned? |
| Rose191: | friend |
| THat: | just a work – a bit bored – we are moving offices next week so i should be sorting out my stuff |

## FORMALITY AND SPOKEN TEXTS

Now that you have looked at formal and informal written texts, you will be aware of just how much variation is possible within written texts. You are now going to focus on two spoken texts with the same idea of contrast and variation.

## Exercise 7

This time, take the two texts together (from Chapters 3 and 1, respectively) and analyse how they compare in terms of formality. Start with vocabulary, but go beyond that to consider any other aspects of language you regard as important.

Suggestions for answer at given the back of the book.

> Ladies and gentlemen, this is a difficult moment for America. I, unfortunately, will be going back to Washington after my remarks. Secretary Rod Paige and the Lt Governor will take the podium and discuss education. I do want to thank the folks here at Booker Elementary School for their hospitality.
>
> Today we've had a national tragedy. Two airplanes have crashed into the World Trade Center in an apparent terrorist attack on our country. I have spoken to the Vice President, to the Governor of New York, to the Director of the FBI, and have ordered that the full resources of the federal government go to help the victims and their families, and to conduct a full-scale investigation to hunt down and to find those folks who committed this act.
>
> Terrorism against our nation will not stand.
>
> And now if you would join me in a moment of silence. May God bless the victims, their families, and America.
>
> Thank you very much.

Key to symbols:    (.) = normal pause
[ ] = vocal effects
**bold** = stressed syllables
| = simultaneous speech
A = Anne
M = Mark

A: hi
M: hi
A: I just been to feed the **cat**
M: oh no
A: he's been out in the **wild wind** (.) and **rain** (.) and he's really **cross** with me
M: **is** he?
A: I **played** with him for a bit (.) until he got **dry**
M: what d'ya give him to **eat**?
A: I gave him **tur**key
M: hasn't he had that last tin of **tu**na yet?
A: no I'm saving it **up** cos (.) we gotta **leave** him **have**n't we (.)
A:          | over the **week**end
M:     | oh **yeah**
A: thought I'd do a bit of     | **bri**bery
M:                 | good **think**ing [*laughter*]
A:                   [*laughter*]

For further work on ideas about formality and informality in social contexts, refer to the companion book in this series, *Language and Social Contexts* by Amanda Coultas.

## SUMMARY

This chapter has looked at formality and informality in written and spoken texts, referring in particular to:

- Aspects of ritual and repertoire
- Lexical variation including reference to semantic fields and archaisms
- Taboo language

It has shown that although aspects of formality and informality can be identified through looking at lexical items in texts, it is also important to look at other aspects of texts such as grammar and graphology.

# CHAPTER 6

# LITERARY AND NON-LITERARY ASPECTS

Throughout English work in secondary school the terms 'literary' and 'non-literary' are used to distinguish between different types of text. The same terms are used in Assessment Objective AO2 of the combined English Language and Literature A Level specifications, which says that candidates must respond to 'literary and non-literary texts'. This extensive official use of the terms suggests that they are accepted ways of describing texts, which everyone understands and is comfortable with. This chapter will explore whether the distinction between the two types of text is in fact as clear-cut as is often thought.

## NON-LITERARY TEXTS

### Exercise 1

Figure 6.1 is the front cover of a leaflet produced for students by the NatWest Bank. The booklet, which is itself part of a series designed for different groups of customers, gives advice about managing money and encourages its readers to use the NatWest Bank. The front cover here shows a fridge door with various notes stuck to it. What features of this text allow it to be labelled as non-literary?

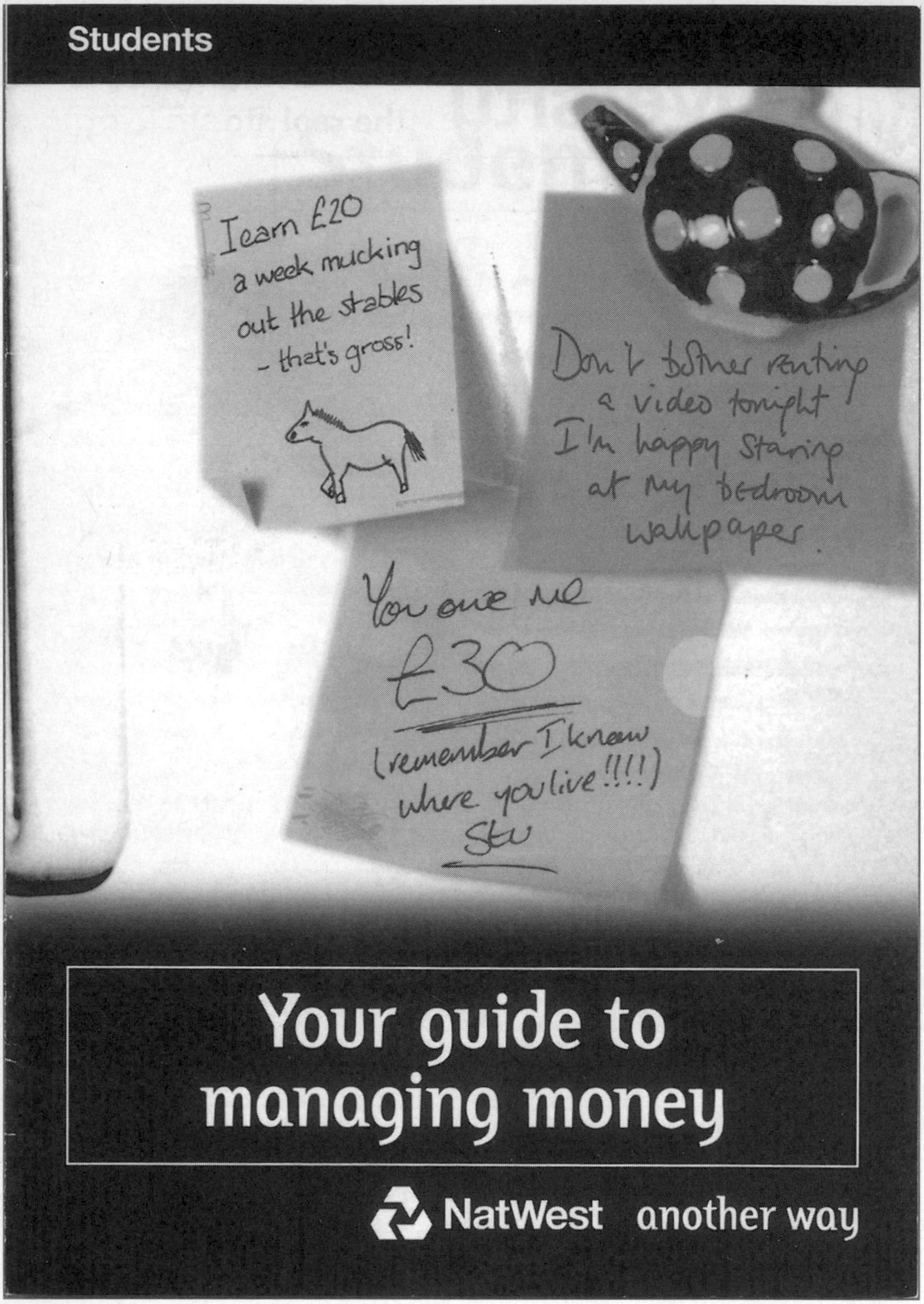


*Figure 6.1* Front cover of Natwest leaflet

## Suggestions for Answer

This text has many of the features which are associated with non-literary texts. It is in the very broad **genre** of advertisements (although it can also be categorised as a guide) and it has a clear functional purpose, to sell student bank accounts. We have no sense of who the author of this text is. It is **ephemeral**, in that it is not meant to last very long; it will probably be replaced the following year with a new campaign.

Like many adverts, it has different constituent parts, some of which are visual, some of which are verbal, and some which are a mixture of the two. The leaflet has at the top an identification of its target audience, 'Students', which also suggests that this is one of a series of leaflets, probably to be placed in racks, each one for a different target group. The most central and dominating image is the representation of a fridge door and the three 'handwritten' notes, each one suggesting aspects of a typical student life-style and each one concerned with an aspect of money. They are linked by the idea that as a student money is always tight, and strategies are needed to cope. One obvious strategy is to read this guide. Another, by implication, is to bank with NatWest.

There is, then, the bank logo, which is followed by a slogan which probably appears on all the booklets in the series.

> To summarise then, someone looking at this text might consider the following as reasons to categorise it as non-literary text:
>
> - It is a form of promotional material, and adverts are always categorised as non-literary
> - It is ephemeral and not meant to last
> - It has no named author
> - It has a clear purpose – to sell bank accounts
> - It contains visual as well as verbal elements
> - It uses varied graphological features such as different font and images
> - It contains a slogan – repeated language also used in other texts from this company
> - It contains brand logos

## LITERARY TEXTS

## Exercise 2

Now look at the poem on page 62. Whereas the advert in Figure 6.1 could be understood without any assistance, this poem requires some context to make it more accessible. The whole point of most adverts is to be seen and understood relatively easily and quickly but literary texts do not always give up their meanings so readily.

## Another Poem About Old Photographs

This one's good. Look closely, you can almost
detect each ridge and whorl of Uncle Tommy's index-
fingerprint. That white curved edge top left – that's
the sky we had in Cork, Nineteen Fifty-Six,

the summer of his first box-camera. This one
I call 'Late Malevich: Town Hall, Macroom',
or, if in a figurative whimsy, 'Klansmen
Routed by Doves in Freak Arkansas Snowstorm'.

It should have been the family group
but Tommy was, by then, flouting convention.
Drunk with Kodakry, he'd wave us round, then swoop –
Duhigs trapped between his cross-sights and the sun,

the Red-faced Baron, hunched behind his black box
which struggled to record his flights of art
on sun-bleached or thumb-benighted film. This next
came out. My mother couldn't believe it.

Plain as sin, my Father's Harris blocks the view
to Gougane Barra from Glengariff Bay.
'The best jacket I ever had,' he'd say,
'No doubt about it. The camera doesn't lie.'

(Ian Duhig, 1990)

Many poets have written poems about photographs, usually finding great significance in what they represent. Ian Duhig's title shows he is aware that he is writing within a genre, but saying that it is 'another' such poem hints that he is going to do something different. The joke of the poem is that the three photos he describes are all duds. The first one has a fingerprint on it, the second is completely white, and the third is meant to be a landscape but is a close-up of his father's tweed jacket. Each dud photo is given a description which makes it out to be better than it really is.

What features of this text allow it to be labelled as 'literary'?

## Suggestions for Answer

This poem has many of the features which are associated with a certain type of literary text. Its layout and design immediately signal that it belongs to the broad genre of poetry: key features are the way it has a title, it uses stanzas, it is written in lines (although these lines do not, like some poems, always begin with capital letters). It also has a named author, and a date has been provided by this book as a further piece of information. Authorship is important for a number of reasons. It suggests that the author wants to be associated with the text, and is in a way proud of it. It helps the readers because they may want to link this poem to others that are by the same author. The date provides a context for the poem, while at the same time suggesting that it is still worth reading. Ironically, perhaps, dating a text like this means that it has more permanence.

Its title, with the reference to 'another poem' places this poem in a sub-genre, poems about photographs. Its first line, meanwhile, makes the reader work hard to establish the context. Unlike the advert, which needs to make everything clear, this is more oblique. We have to work out the fictional story-line that the narrator of the poem is showing some family photos to other people. The many **proper nouns**, describing people and Irish places, are not explained for us. We also have to work out the main 'joke' of the poem – that far from being 'good', the photos are in fact duds.

The first line of the poem sounds as if we have joined a conversation in the middle; the words 'this one' suggesting that there have been others already. In addition to the **narrator** of the poem, who is in the fictional situation of showing the photographs, in the first line there is reference to a **narratee**, a 'you' who is being shown the photographs. Within the fictional story that is being told, this could be a member of the family, or a constructed reader, or indeed both at the same time.

Just as titles and first lines are especially important in poems, so are last lines. The final statement, that the 'camera doesn't lie', is left hanging to make us think. It could be ironic given what we have been told about the photos being so bad, or it could be questioning the assumption made by this common phrase; visual representation is not always as truthful as we sometimes think. However we interpret this line, the key point here is the poem ends on a note of **ambiguity**. Whereas the advert aims to make its message clear, the poem has more than one potential meaning.

Another feature of this text is the *creativity* of its language. The author invents the word 'Kodakry' and, using **metaphors**, makes a link between the photographer and the famous World War I fighter pilot the Red Baron. The titles of the completely blank photo in the second stanza also play with ideas of abstract art and images of whiteness – Ku Klux Klansmen who wear white robes, doves and snow put together make just a white blank.

To summarise then, someone looking at this text might consider the following as reasons to categorise it as literary text:

- It belongs to a recognisable genre poetry, and poetry is nearly always viewed as literature
- It has named authorship and is dated when reproduced, so giving a degree of permanence
- It is more ambiguous in its meanings and makes the reader work hard to find them
- Its organisation has some visual as well as verbal elements
- It has a narrative structure with a narrator and a narratee
- It uses language in a creative way, including metaphor
- Its purpose is not transparent

## NON-LITERARY/LITERARY TEXTS: ARE THEY COMPLETELY DIFFERENT?

The features identified earlier in the NatWest text in Figure 6.1 were what most readers would expect to find in this sort of non-literary text. There are, however, some other features which are not always thought of as belonging to such texts.

If you look again at Figure 6.1 you will notice that it has a clear sense of **narrative**. The text addresses you the potential reader ('your money'). This narratee, or created reader, is not really 'you' but a created version of a certain typical reader. This typical reader is a student with money problems who wants help. Note too how each of the notes on the fridge door tells a different story within the overall story – there are a number of voices which 'speak' in this text. It would be relatively straight-forward to write a story or play based on the mini-stories we have here. This text is tightly organised with each section contributing to the narrative as a whole.

Notice too that the advert uses ambiguity to make its point. The slogan 'another way' is left deliberately vague, inviting the reader to work out its possible meanings.

So if we look at both Figure 6.1 and the poem together we can see that there are some qualities shared by them. These are:

- They both belong to a recognisable genre but these genres are conventionally given different status
- Both have visual aspects to their organisation
- They both use creative ideas around language
- They both have a sense of narrative, with a narrator(s) and a narratee
- Both texts have a degree of ambiguity, requiring work from the reader

Meanwhile the features which most distinguish their difference are:

- The NatWest text is ephemeral and not meant to last, the poem is more permanent
- The NatWest text has a transparent purpose, the poem less so

The terms literary and non-literary set up an idea of opposites. What is established from this initial exploration of just two texts, though, is that the two categories under discussion are not as distinctly separate as is sometimes suggested. This will now be explored further.

## VALUE TERMS

The terms literary and non-literary are often used in **collocation**; this means that they appear frequently together and in the same word order. Although it is not necessarily the case that pairs of words in collocation always place the most important word first, the fact that 'literary' comes first is probably significant. This significance is increased when you consider that the term 'non-literary' is **marked**. When a word or phrase is marked, it means that it is signified as being different from the norm. In this case there are literary texts, and then there are other texts which are not literary, but which have no other positive term of their own. The effect of this would seem to be that literary texts are seen as being the more important texts and thus as more valued.

This idea of some texts being more valued than others, however, works also *within* the category of literary texts. So some literary texts are more highly valued than others in the same category. This distinction is often made by naming authors, rather than specific texts. The school National Curriculum, for example, gives lists of major writers with well-established critical reputations who have produced works of high quality. Top of this list comes Shakespeare, who is a compulsory author at all key stages in English from age 11 onwards. Indeed so eminent is Shakespeare that his name and his works are synonymous – we study Shakespeare.

Meanwhile texts such as personal diaries and travel writing, which in most cases are seen as non-literary, are sometimes elevated to the status of literature if they are deemed to be of a superior quality to their supposedly run of the mill counterparts. What is it that lifts these texts into the category of literature? Adapting slightly the features of literary texts noted when we looked at Ian Duhig's poem, the following features seem to apply to texts that are given the status of being literary:

- They are written by authors who have a critical reputation
- They are written in forms which are seen as literary, poetry always so, diaries sometimes
- They are complex in their ideas and/or structure
- They contain serious and important ideas
- They are notable for their use of language, which is often in some way innovative
- Their purposes go beyond the transparent

If we are trying to define the essential qualities of a literary text, all of these features need to be investigated further. In the first, having a critical reputation depends upon the views of a select group of people. In the second, if the form in which the text is written is seen as literary, this involves a sort of pre-judgement. The next three are all based ultimately on subjective judgements, because there is no scientific formula which defines complexity, seriousness or linguistic innovation. It may well be that these judgements are endorsed by lots of influential people, such as critics, but the fact remains that they are judgements, not absolute statements. As for the final point – the purpose of literary texts – they are as much involved in commercial selling processes as any other sort of text, even if they are sometimes not quite so open about it.

## Exercise 3

Place the following texts into one of three columns: Literature, Not Literature, Not Sure. Once you have done this, justify your choices. There is no commentary with this exercise.

*Hamlet* by William Shakespeare
*Hamlet the Mouse* – a children's story
A novel published by Mills & Boon
An unpublished script for *EastEnders*
A published script for *The Royle Family*
Rap lyrics reproduced on a CD cover
Lyrics by Bob Dylan published in a separate volume
The Bible
A biography of Princess Diana
*Timebends* – an autobiography by the playwright Arthur Miller
An American crime novel
A previously unpublished poem by Wordsworth that has just been discovered

The status of literary texts, then, is based ultimately on opinion, opinion which is usually underpinned by long-standing reputation. Jeremy Paxman, writing in the *Independent on Sunday*, 7 February 1999, told the story of a friend's teenage son, who was studying Bill Bryson's travel book *Notes from a Small Island* for A Level:

His teenage son who is studying for his English A Level, arrived home the other day with Bryson's *Notes from a Small Island* under his arm. As the boy is something of a stranger to reading for pleasure, my friend was delighted that he seemed to have decided of his own accord to spend a few hours inside a book. He was wrong. Bill Bryson was one of his set books for his A Level. Of all the works produced in the richest language and richest literary tradition in the world, the education authorities have chosen to make students apply themselves to a book which week after week sits there in the best-seller lists.

> There is nothing wrong with *Notes from a Small Island*. But even Bill Bryson wouldn't claim it was up there with Shakespeare, Dickens or even Trollope. Doubtless, examination boards will have some excuse. Probably something to do with encouraging people to read.

Paxman's argument can be broken down as follows:

- There is a difference between reading for pleasure and reading for A Level exams
- Popular best-sellers should not be studied seriously
- The English language has a great literary tradition
- This tradition contains great authors who are 'above' writers like Bryson
- Encouraging people to read is not a reason for choosing A Level texts

There are, however, assumptions here which can be questioned. Shouldn't reading at A Level involve pleasure and the encouragement to read widely? Are best-sellers of limited quality, simply because they are read by lots of people? (Shakespeare, Dickens and Trollope were all exceptionally popular in their own lifetimes.) How can students develop their own critical views if they are told in advance that books are 'great'?

So, although the term 'literary text' is frequently applied and frequently accepted, it has to be challenged as being at least in part a matter of taste and convention. It is a term which as much reflects social values and traditions as it does formal analysis. And as has been seen in the analysis of texts so far, many of the qualities possessed by literary texts are shared by non-literary texts too, and vice versa.

What we are faced with, then, is two terms that are rather more problematic than first seemed the case. To call a text a *literary text* involves keying in to social and cultural values that are impossible to define. To call a text a *non-literary text* pre-determines what it is not, rather than what it is. Looking at the examples we have used so far, what we can say in a very broad way is that both are texts, and in a more precise categorisation we can say that one text is an advert and one a poem. Within those two categories they have some qualities which are similar and some which are different. Although the terms literary and non-literary can be applied to the texts because of certain features, they have other features in common which make the terms less useful.

## Exercise 4

*Travels with a Donkey* by R.L. Stevenson (1879), *Notes from a Small Island* by Bill Bryson (1995), *Club 18–30 brochure* (2000)

*Travels with a Donkey* is a travel book in which Stevenson describes a trip through the Cévennes in France which he undertook with a donkey called Modestine. One of the book's running jokes is that the donkey is a strong-willed and stubborn creature which is intended to make the journey easy but in fact makes it difficult. Stevenson is best known for his novels *Dr Jekyll and Mr Hyde*, *Treasure Island* and *Kidnapped*.

Bill Bryson is an American who travelled round Britain alone, and recorded his impressions in *Notes from a Small Island*. The book's popularity is referred to in the article by Jeremy Paxman on pages 66 and 67.

*Club 18–30* is a travel company specialising in holidays for young people. Their holidays have a reputation for sun, sex, booze and sand, an image that they cultivate in their brochure. This text, unlike the other two, was printed in colour and surrounded by photographs.

These three texts are connected by topic – they are all in some way or another about foreign travel. They also have other similarities and differences. Bearing in mind the work done in this chapter so far, answer the following questions:

1. In what ways can these texts be seen as similar and in what ways different? Consider in particular:

   (a) the purposes and audiences for each text;
   (b) how each text is organised around concepts of time;
   (c) how each text has a distinctive narrative voice which 'speaks' the text.

2. How does your answer to the question above show that the distinction between literary and non-literary texts is not always as obvious as is often suggested?

Suggestions for answer are given at the back of the book.

---

### *Travels with a Donkey* by R.L. Stevenson (1879)

The next day (Tuesday, September 24th), it was two o'clock in the afternoon before I got my journal written up and my knapsack repaired, for I was determined to carry my knapsack in the future and have no more ado with baskets; and half an hour afterwards I set out for Le Cheylard l'Evêque, a place on the borders of the forest of Mercoire. A man, I was told, should walk there in an hour and a half; and I thought it scarce too ambitious to suppose that a man encumbered with a donkey might cover the same distance in four hours . . .

There was no direct road to Cheylard, and it was no easy affair to make a passage in this uneven country and through this intermittent labyrinth of tracks. It must have been about four when I struck Sagnerousse, and went on my way rejoicing in a sure point of departure. Two hours afterwards, the dusk rapidly falling, in a lull of the wind, I issued from a fir-wood where I had long been wandering, and found, not the looked-for village, but another marish bottom among rough-and-tumble hills.

For some time past I had heard the ringing of cattle-bells ahead; and now, as I came out of the skirts of the wood, I saw near upon a dozen cows and perhaps as many more black figures, which I conjectured to be children, although the mist had almost unrecognisably exaggerated their forms. These were all silently following each other round and round in a circle, now taking hands, now breaking up with chains and reverences. A dance of children appeals to very innocent and lively thoughts; but, at nightfall on the marshes, the thing was eerie and fantastic to behold. Even I, who am well enough read in Herbert Spencer, felt a sort of silence fall for an instant on my mind.

The next, I was pricking Modestine forward, and guiding her like an unruly ship through the open. In a path, she went doggedly ahead of her own accord, as before a fair wind; but once on the turf or among heather, and the brute became demented. The tendency of lost travellers to go round in a circle was developed in her to the degree of passion, and it took all the steering I had in me to keep even a decently straight course through a single field. While I was thus desperately tacking through the bog, children and cattle began to disperse, until only a pair of girls remained behind. From these I sought direction on my path.

The peasantry in general were but little disposed to counsel a wayfarer. One old devil simply retired into his house, and barricaded the door on my approach; and I might beat and shout myself hoarse, he turned a deaf ear. Another, having given me a direction which, as I found afterwards, I had misunderstood, complacently watched me going wrong without adding a sign. He did not care a stalk of parsley if I wandered all night upon the hills! As for these two girls, they were a pair of impudent sly sluts, with not a thought but mischief. One put out her tongue at me, the other bade me follow the cows; and they both giggled and jogged each other's elbows. The Beast of Gevaudan ate about a hundred children of this district; I began to think of him with sympathy.

In this extract Bryson has travelled to Bournemouth:

### *Notes from a Small Island* by Bill Bryson (1995)

By the time I reached the East Cliff, a neighbourhood of medium-sized hotels perched high above a black sea, I was soaked through and muttering. The one thing to be said for Bournemouth is that you are certainly spoiled for choice with hotels. Among the many gleaming palaces of comfort that lined every street for blocks around, I selected an establishment on a side-street for no other reason than that I liked its sign: neat capitals in pink neon glowing beckoningly through the slicing rain. I stepped inside, shedding water, and could see at a glance it was a good choice – clean, nicely old-fashioned,

*continued*

attractively priced at £26 B&B according to the notice on the wall, and with the kind of smothering warmth that makes your glasses steam and brings on sneezing fits. I decanted several ounces of water from my sleeve and asked for a single room for two nights.

'Is it raining out?' the reception girl asked brightly as I filled in the registration card between sneezes and pauses to wipe water from my face with the back of my arm.

'No, my ship sank and I had to swim the last seven miles.'

'Oh yes?' she went on in a manner that made me suspect she was not attending my words closely. 'And will you be dining with us tonight, Mr – ' she glanced at my water-smeared card 'Mr Brylcreem?' I considered the alternative – a long slog through stair-rods of rain – and felt inclined to stay in. Besides, between her cheerily bean-sized brain and my smeared scrawl, there was every chance they would charge the meal to another room. I said I'd eat in, accepted a key and drippingly found my way to my room.

### Club 18–30

Trabukos Beach Club Kavos

A get away from it all holiday it's most definitely NOT. It's total in yer face non-stop Kavos for those with serious stamina committed to the God of party. With some apartments in the surrounding area, it's always right in the middle of the action. The beach is only a couple of minutes away, and if that's too far for your head to handle there's a great big pool – the main hang out in Kavos, with a fab poolside bar that rocks all day. '42nd Street' has everything it takes to party and serves as base camp nightlife before we hit the bars and clubs right on the doorstep, including the famous Buzz party bar. Even though life's no rehearsal this is one for the fearless and the extreme. All B&B rooms are simply furnished, sleep 2, and have private facilities and fridge, most with a balcony. The self catering studios and apartments sleep 2 or 2–4 with a kitchenette, private facilities and balcony or terrace.

## SUMMARY

Although texts are often labelled as literary or non-literary, these distinctions are not always very helpful. This chapter shows that so-called non-literary texts can contain the narrative features and linguistic creativity often associated with literature texts only. Meanwhile literary texts are often given this label simply because of the author's status.

In the previous chapters pairs of terms have been seen as limited in their distinctions once a more sophisticated analysis has been applied. In the case of 'literary' and 'non-literary', however, the distinction is based upon presupposition rather than the quality of analysis.

# SUGGESTIONS FOR ANSWER

## CHAPTER 1, EXERCISE 3

The image of the cocktail glass works alongside the hook line to refer to the fictional spy character, James Bond. Note the small details of the image, such as the cocktail-stick sword, symbolic of a swashbuckling fighter. Think how different the image might seem if the stick had a cartoon character such as Mickey Mouse on the end of it.

The dry martini cocktail is Bond's regular drink, which he orders 'shaken, not stirred'. The hook line reverses the wording of this, producing 'stirred, not shaken'. In this reversed form, the phrase can suggest, not just the idea of a method for mixing drinks, but the human experiences of being emotionally affected ('stirred') yet not unsettled ('not shaken').

The text is advertising for an executive director in a council, not a spy. But it is suggesting that the person who gets the job will share many qualities with a figure such as Bond. This idea is established through extensive references to the semantic field of intelligence work: 'nerve', 'cool and confident [manager] with a steady hand', 'a licence to thrill', 'accomplished troubleshooter whose aim is deadly', 'targeting', 'agent', all of which terms are also used to apply to council work. In addressing the reader in this way, the text establishes a narratee who is a bold and intrepid man.

It is difficult to describe the order you used to make sense of the text precisely, because everyone will have their own way of scanning the text. However, because the approach of this text is unusual – public sector jobs are rarely seen as this exciting – you may well have checked out its source in order to find out whether it was serious or not. This would mean scanning the bottom of the advert for the employer's name, for example. Something else you might have done to validate the ad is look at the mailing address and other contact details.

It is likely that you registered the image but held it a little in suspension until you read the hook line. You then probably went back to the image and re-registered it.

## CHAPTER 2, EXERCISE 5

Looking at this text as a piece of writing on the page, there are several aspects which suggest spontaneity. Spelling sometimes goes unchecked ('arpund' instead of 'around') but is at one point self-corrected by Rose191 ('firned'/'friend'), capital letters are omitted at the beginning of utterances and for the name 'david', **homophones** replace words ('what r u up to?'), and punctuation is used irregularly (sometimes questions marks are used, sometimes not). Although the text is saved by the computer, and so there is a permanent record kept, strict technical accuracy does not seem to be especially important to the two people.

Looking at the text as an exchange between two people, there are also several aspects which suggest spontaneity: the way topics are introduced and changed, along with considerable pragmatic understanding between the two, show features similar to spontaneous talk. THat's 'hello stranger' is more than a greeting, it is a statement or accusation that her friend has missed yoga. This allows her to mention the class without any formal setting out of the agenda. When Rose191 attempts to change the topic by mentioning her article, and then asks 'what r u up to?', the topic change is at first ignored before finally being responded to at the end of this extract.

It has already been noted, however, that apparently spontaneous conversation follows certain 'scripts' and it is clear here that these two people know each other reasonably well and go through certain routines that would be expected of friends who have not seen each other for a while. They write about what they have been doing recently, what they might do over Easter and other future plans. It is also worth looking at the way turns are taken. Unlike actual talk, the technology does not allow overlaps where both 'speak' at once. This means that whole utterances need to be planned, written and then delivered. When Rose191 takes three turns in a row, this is probably because THat is composing a quite long turn beginning 'it was really good though'. While Rose191 has changed the topic, her friend is completing what she had started earlier, and it takes her a while before she eventually answers. This suggests that although the overall conversation is relatively unplanned, within the conversation planning is required.

When looked at in this way, chatroom dialogue is a sophisticated mixture of features taken from what were once seen as the very separate worlds of writing and speaking. It would be inappropriate to say that the chat in this text is either planned or unplanned – it has elements of spontaneity, learned routines and short-term planning.

## CHAPTER 2, EXERCISE 7

The call-centre worker's speech (W) shows a relatively high level of formality and organisation, both of which suggest that he is reading from a screen something that has been written down for him as a script. The relatively few false starts, repetitions and pauses all suggest a fluency not normally encountered in spontaneous talk. There is also a strong sense that W needs to continue with the script regardless of what P says. When P says 'pardon' (perhaps as a polite way of registering shock that he has committed himself to 'just 5 or 6 minutes') W ignores him and continues to ask for his name.

As the interview progresses, W asks questions which demand certain sorts of answer so that they can be put into the computer. 'How satisfied or dissatisfied were you with the service' sounds a relatively open question, and P says it was 'fine'. This, however, is not exact enough for the computer script, so W provides three options for him to choose from. It takes P two goes to get there, but in the end he provides an answer which fits the script.

As the conversation progresses, W becomes more and more forceful in his demands. Although we do not know how W actually says the words, 'you tell me whether you agree or disagree' sounds increasingly like a command. Now he is involved in the conversation, P cannot get out, and W is happy to feed him his lines – 'and the instructions were clear and easy to follow'. There are times when P tentatively tries to take the conversation away from the script – when he says 'ultimately' he is suggesting some delay – but W chooses to ignore this as he continues inexorably with the script.

In terms of planning, then, W's talk is highly planned, and he has well-rehearsed strategies to deal with P if he wanders off the script. P does occasionally try to do this, but he is soon brought back to where he should be. Although he is not aware of it, P is also taking his part in a very planned speech event.

The effect of all this is that it allows the production of data which can be computer-analysed. Whether it actually reflects what the customer thinks is more open to question.

## CHAPTER 3, EXERCISE 6

It should be clear here that Krogstad has lent Nora some money and that she is therefore in his debt both literally and possibly in other ways too. If her husband was ill at the time, then he probably does not know about the debt, so she is working behind his back, even if it was done for his sake in the first place. We can also work out from the way the conversation is structured that Krogstad is going to accuse Nora of something. Did her father really sign the document or did she forge his signature? And if this is the case, he is then in a position to blackmail her.

We can work this out because the conversation has been written with us (or us as a live audience) in mind. The careful retelling of past events is so that we can work out the story. In the real world, it would be highly unlikely that two people would go over the past in such a clear and **chronological** way. In addition to understanding what has happened in the fictional past, we can also work out the motives of the characters at this point. Krogstad is playing a game with Nora, luring her into telling lies before he discloses what he knows. She is desperately trying to cover up what she fears is to be uncovered.

These are the motives of those inside the play. But what of Ibsen's purposes as author of the play? One purpose is to entertain his audience with a story and characters which interest them. There could be other purposes though. Although it would be hard to say anything conclusive from such a short extract, we can work out some possibilities. In most cultural circumstances the individual money-lender is represented as a villain, and we get a sense that Nora is being unjustifiably bullied by this man. Potentially, then, Ibsen is informing us about aspects of social injustice, especially when Nora's motives are so noble. And with this informative function comes a persuasive one too – in siding with Nora we are being urged to consider the role of a woman who is trapped, and whether social injustice needs to be challenged. To test out these theories, you could read the whole of the play.

## CHAPTER 3, EXERCISE 7

The various labels at the top of Figure 3.1 show that this is a complicated text in terms of its genre – and thus also in its purposes. At the very top of the text is the identification that it appears in a newspaper, on a given day and date. Below this, though, and in the centre of the text is the word 'advertisement'. Adverts in papers are not usually labelled in this way, because it is usually self-evident that this is what they are. This text has been labelled as an advertisement, though, because otherwise it could be confused with an actual news story. Much of the text does indeed look like the rest of the paper, so in order to make it clear what sort of text this is, and who has produced it, it is labelled as an 'advertisement'. This is reinforced by the side panel which says 'content supplied by' and then the Nexus logo. The confusion is potentially made even greater by the fact that the story about the Metro is in a newspaper with the same name.

So far, then, we have a text which as an advert has persuasive qualities, while its logo will be part of another selling process via brand identity. There is also a suggestion, though, that this is an informative text if it looks like a newspaper article, and this idea of information is again identified in the text, this time by the words 'News and Information'. The two labels 'Advertisement' and 'News and Information' seem at first glance to contradict each other, but in fact make perfect sense within this context.

The main story in the body of the text is that the Metro advertising team have won a marketing competition. In one sense, then, this is indeed an informative news story, but to illustrate the story the winning adverts are shown. These six adverts both illustrate the news and again operate as persuasive texts in their own right. Part of their original persuasivenenss, however, and the reason they won the competition is their verbal cleverness. As readers we have to work out that each advert plays with the idea of leading brands of petrol. In this sense, then, they are entertaining readers with their verbal play.

Even the story itself can be seen to have a triple purpose. While on the surface it informs us of a competition success, it also persuades us of the success and skills of the Marketing Team who have raised revenue while working on a tiny budget. Meanwhile the story has been presented in such a way, with its use of puns – 'paid off' – and highlighted quotation, to entertain us enough to read on to the end.

To readers of the *Metro* newspaper, many of whom would have been travelling on the Metro train as they read this, it was no doubt a straightforward enough text. But to us as analysers of text it shows how subtle a process it can be to identify the real purposes behind what we read.

## CHAPTER 5, EXERCISE 6

Lexically, the participants use very little by way of specialist vocabulary, even though they are referring to an activity (yoga) that does have its own semantic field. While their yoga teacher may well use specialist lexis when teaching the moves, these chatroom users are not instructing each other, but rather 'checking in' with each other after the absence of one of them from class. In fact, you could see THat's use of 'we were jumping arpund all over the shop' as a way of deliberately avoiding specialist usage, in order to reassure Rose191 that she hasn't missed out on any new knowledge.

As was noted in the earlier suggestions for answer (Chapter 2, page 74), use of non-standard spelling, lower case, tolerance of typos and use of abbreviated forms are all related to the need for speed in this new interactive context and are likely to become the convention in this genre rather than forms of rule-breaking. However, the nature of the relationship between participants is as important here as the genre being used: with only two participants in the chatroom, it would be perfectly possible to use very formal language with none of the features mentioned above in evidence. Informality is therefore, in this case, as much a signal of friendship and intimacy between participants as an obligatory feature of the genre.

The participants use words and phrases that are common in informal spoken contexts where speakers feel free to call on aspects of regional identity: both chatroom users are from the north of England and this may explain 'dead hard' and, perhaps, 'all over the shop'. Other aspects of colloquial language are more universal: 'i'm knackered', 'the same call', 'a funny old', 'teacher's pet'. The chatroom language doesn't have the precision of the legal document. In fact, casual conversation needs a level of deliberate vagueness in order to work (Channel, 1994), and you can see this in action here with items such as 'a lot', 'about 6', 'a bit' (used twice), 'next week'. Idiomatic language – such as 'my legs are killing' and 'hello stranger' – is, like vague language, not meant to be pinned down in any literal sense. THat doesn't literally mean that her legs are killing her; nor is she saying that she has never met her friend. Idiomatic language only works because we don't take it at face value; it is very different, therefore, from the language used in the legal text.

The chatroom is also very different from the will grammatically. Participants see no problem with incompleteness – such as 'my legs are killing', 'a bit bored' – or minor sentences, such as 'ok'. This situation is very different from that of the legal document, where sentences are very long and involve many parentheses and sub-clauses. The grammatical **cohesion** of the legal document requires the reader to be able to scan several lines in order to make the required links: for example, see how, in Section 6, the items in brackets towards the end of the text refer back to the first line of that section.

The chatroom, however, is complex in other ways. If you read the earlier suggestions for answer (Chapter 2, page 74), you will be reminded of how complex the turn-taking procedures are in this type of communication. Chatrooms are not simple texts; but, with an average line length of six words (Werry, 1996), their complexity is between turns rather than within them.

## CHAPTER 5, EXERCISE 7

One of the most obvious differences in lexical formality is in the use of terms for addressing and naming. In the casual conversation in the transcript, the speakers know each other well and do not need any address terms; nor do they need to name the cat or identify where Anne has been. Their environment is a known factor, and it is only in mediated texts such as radio soap operas and pieces of literary fiction that the reader has to be informed constantly about what is going on. The assumptions that people can or cannot make about shared knowledge is an area known in linguistics as pragmatics.

As was noted in the earlier suggestions for answer (Chapter 3, pages 30 to 31), George Bush's speech is heavily mediated as a result of having several audiences simultaneously: the people in the school, American TV viewers, TV viewers world-wide. Because of this, his addressing and naming practices are very formal and explicit:

Ladies and gentlemen
Secretary Rod Paige and the Lieutenant Governor
Booker Elementary School
the World Trade Center
the Vice President
the Governor of New York
the Director of the FBI

In the casual conversation, the speakers simply use 'hi' to each other.

The differences above are the direct result of the different pragmatics of the two texts. Everything that George Bush says has to be self-sufficient and make complete sense to several audiences, while Anne and Mark have their own realities that do not need to be made explicit, because they have conversations for themselves and not for an audience of millions. If they did have a further audience, that audience would need to know all sorts of things in order to make sense of the language used, for example, that the cat in question is not their own, that Anne has been to a neighbour's house to feed it, that it has been badly behaved. So, when Mark says 'oh no', he really means 'I hope you had an ok time and the cat behaved himself' (see the earlier suggestions for answer on this text in Chapter 1, page 9).

Even though the George Bush speech is not the most formal text of its type you could find, it does use more abstract or complex vocabulary than is the norm for everyday interactions: for example, 'remarks', 'podium', 'hospitality', 'tragedy', 'resources', 'conduct', 'committed', 'nation', 'terrorism'. In contrast, the casual conversation uses very concrete or simple references, such as 'cat', 'wind', 'rain', 'cross'. The mild connotations of the term 'cross' suit the topic of the cat's attitude, but would be totally inappropriate as a response to the events of 11 September. Bush's task is to reflect the scale of the disaster, and formal abstract terms such as 'tragedy' are more suited to that task. As was noted in the earlier suggestions for answer on pages 30 and 31, the term 'folks' to describe the terrorists strikes a rather inappropriately homey note alongside the other, more formal, terms used.

Bush needs to create and maintain a sense of gravity, so any examples of vague language or humour are inappropriate. The nearest Bush gets to a piece of vague language is the term 'moment', when he asks for silence. However, while 'moment' might be a vague term, it does have connotations of importance: we say 'it was a momentous occasion', when we want to imply that an event was grand and memorable. In contrast, the speakers in the casual conversation use the vague phrases 'for a bit' and 'a bit of bribery'. Imagine George Bush saying 'And now please join me for a bit of silence'.

Just as Bush's opening is a formal greeting, so his closing is a formal expression of thanks: 'thank you very much', rather than 'thanks'. Any such abbreviation would be seen as too informal, as would shortenings of words or grammatical ellipsis; for example, there is no equivalent of Anne's 'cos' or 'I just been'.

Finally, you need to remember that because these two texts are speech transferred from a visual and oral/aural context to the page, they are representations. In both cases, nearly all of the prosodic and paralinguistic information has been lost, information which itself carries many indications of formality or informality. The laughter of Anne and Mark, their enjoyment of each other's performance of speech, the seriousness of Bush's face and the groups of concerned state and military personnel surrounding him – all these aspects of each scene work alongside speech to convey a richer meaning than ever can be represented on the page.


## CHAPTER 6, EXERCISE 4

The purpose of the Club 18–30 text is more obvious than those of the other two texts. The fact that it is a form of advertising, and therefore designed to sell something, means it can be labelled a non-literary text if the definitions used at the beginning of the chapter are applied. It also has a more clearly defined audience than the other texts. Not only is it addressing people who are looking for a holiday, it defines their age too: the organisation is called Club 18–30. This audience is a constructed audience. The term 'constructed' refers to the way an ideal reader or narratee is seen as reading the text – adverts often try to make real readers see themselves in a certain way. So here 18–30-year-olds like to party, have fun, live life to its limits.

The purpose of the travel texts by Stevenson and Bryson is more difficult to define. They are in some ways information texts, yet someone wanting detailed information about the places visited would feel that there are not enough facts. They seem more concerned with personal experience than with geographical detail. They also have a much less clearly defined sense of audience. Although they are written to be read by others, these others are not addressed directly. These texts, then, have a number of features which would suggest that they are literary texts, and, as will be seen shortly, they have many of the narrative features associated with story-telling. Yet, on one level, they are not stories, but accounts of actual experience. This means that they are a sort of hybrid genre, being non-literary in their description of 'real' people and places, yet literary in many other ways. The problem with placing this sort of writing in a convenient category is probably one reason for Jeremy Paxman's concern at Bill Bryson being studied at A Level.

Although the Stevenson and Bryson texts are in many ways very similar, there is one reason why the Stevenson text is more likely to be labelled a literary text. This has nothing as such to do with any analysis of the text, but is part of the process whereby authors are received into what is sometimes called the **literary canon**. The canon refers to authors and their works which are unquestioningly said to possess literary merit. R.L. Stevenson is seen as a literary 'great', so by this process, albeit a questionable one, all of his works are seen as being not only literary, but part of Literature. It is unlikely that Paxman would have objected to Stevenson as part of an A Level course.

One aspect that all the texts share is the way that the narrative of each text is arranged around time. This is, of course, to be expected with travel writing. Whereas other genres of writing, especially fiction, can use time in a non-linear, non-chronological way, travel writing requires that each day is taken in strict sequence of the events happening.

Briefly, some aspects of time to note in the Stevenson text are:

- The mention of precise details at the start of this extract
- The predicted time of the journey with and without donkey
- The time check after two hours of travelling
- The references to 'for some time' and to 'while I was thus desperately tacking'
- The way in which the whole extract has the sequence of starting, travelling, getting lost, seeking shelter

The Bryson text starts slightly later in this process because Bryson has almost arrived at his resting place when this extract begins. The extract begins with a specific reference to time and ends with Bryson going to his room. He can then do one of two things, either shut the door on the reader and start a new day or take the reader into the room with him.

At first sight the Club 18–30 text is again different from the other two texts. Travel brochures, however, need to give prospective buyers an idea what the holiday will be like, and one way of doing this is to suggest a typical day. We are told that the action is 'non-stop'. We then have the daytime action at the beach/pool, the early evening action at the base-camp bar, followed by serious action all night. Although we are given details of rooms, there is strong sense that this is 24-hour living.

It is tempting to say that the Stevenson and Bryson texts are non-fiction texts, because Stevenson and Bryson both existed and both actually made these journeys. There are, however, too many features that are like fiction to allow the non-fiction category to stand unchallenged. Again, these texts are a sort of hybrid. In both texts the authors have constructed themselves as characters in a narrative, a narrative which is, as we have just seen, shaped in part by time. Stevenson presents himself as a writer, as long-suffering, as well read, as a thinker but also as a man who can only take so much – being laughed at by the girls makes him think devious thoughts even if he does not act upon them. Bryson constructs himself as long-suffering, witty, calculating and devious. His basic decency is also challenged by what he sees as unhelpful behaviour. Above all, though, both narrators are constructed as essentially intelligent men, who are outsiders in a strange world.

The Club 18–30 text does not have an identified character as narrator, but it does have a clear and distinctive voice which speaks the text. This voice belongs to someone who knows the place and knows the readers and what they want. The pronoun 'we' has a telling impact here. This is the voice of someone who is on holiday with us. Although this account is just one of many in the brochure, there is a fictional assumption that we are all there together, having a great time. Our narrator even philosophises about life, in the way Stevenson and Bryson do – life, we are told, is not a rehearsal.

It should be clear from the analysis above that the terms literary and non-literary are of limited value when categorising these three texts about travel. Despite being an advert, the Club 18–30 text has much in common with the Stevenson and Bryson texts. This fact alone would suggest that to call a text either literary or non-literary, and to leave it at that, leaves a number of issues unresolved.

# REFERENCES

Baron, N. (2000) *Alphabet to Email*, London: Routledge.

Beard, A. (2003) *The Language of Literature*, London: Routledge.

Channell, J. (1994) *Vague Language*, Oxford: Oxford University Press.

Coultas, A. (2003) *Language and Social Contexts*, London: Routledge.

Werry, C. (1996) 'Linguistic and interactional features of Internet Relay Chat', in S. Herring (ed.) *Computer-mediated Communication*, Amsterdam: John Benjamins.

# GLOSSARY

**Ambiguity**   The prefix 'ambi' literally means 'both'. Ambiguity with reference to textual analysis refers to the idea that texts can have more than one meaning and that these meanings can co-exist

**Arbitrary system**   This refers to the fact that there is no real connection between items of language and the objects named by language

**Archaism**   An archaism is an 'old' word which has largely gone out of everyday use

**Body copy**   This is the main written part of an advertising text rather than the slogan, hook, etc.

**Chronological**   A chronological narrative is when a story is told in the time sequence in which events 'occur'

**Cohesion**   A term which refers to the pattterns of language created within a text which lead to its overall organisation

**Collocation**   This is the way certain words frequently appear together, often in a certain order

**Connotation**   The connotations of a word are the associations it creates. Connotations can be individual but also cultural

**Context**   Literally 'with the text'. Context looks at the circumstances which affect the production of the text by an author and the circumstances that affect the reception of the text by readers

**Deictic reference**   Deictics are words which act as pointers, either forwards, backwards or even outside the text. They serve to situate a speaker or writer in relation to what is said

**Discourse**   Discourse is used in various ways. It can refer to a continuous piece of written or spoken text, but as used in this book it refers to more than this. Here it refers to the way texts cohere or hold together and the ways in which readers recognise this process

**Dysphemism**   The opposite of euphemism – the use of a word or phrase which could be deemed offensive by some

**Ephemeral**   A text that is soon discarded or forgotten can be described as ephemeral

**Etymology**   Etymology looks at the origins of words

**Euphemism**   This is the use of a mild word or phrase instead of one which carries more force in its meaning

**Genre**   Genre refers to an identifiable text-type. It can be used in a number of ways: to identify a type of writing as in a report, a letter, a poem; and it can identify a group of texts which have subject matter in common as in crime fiction, travel writing, sports writing. Sub-genre is a branch of a genre, so if the genre is crime fiction, then police procedural is a sub-genre

**Graphology**   This involves analysing how the appearance of a text affects the ways in which it is read and understood

**Homophones**   Words with the same pronunciation

**Hook**   A hook is rather like a newspaper headline in that it is part of an advert that is designed to catch the reader's attention

**Lexis**   Single words or items of vocabulary

**Literary canon**   Authors and works of literature whose qualities are said to be so great that they belong to an elite group

**Marked**   If a term is said to be marked, this is because it indicates that it is not the norm i.e. 'waitress' is marked by the -*ess* showing a female waiter

**Metaphor**   A word or a phrase which establishes a comparison or analogy between one object or idea and another. 'The game exploded into life' compares a football game with a bomb, for instance

**Modifier**   A modifier is a word or phrase which modifies – or adds to – a noun

**Multimodal**   Multimodal texts have different types of communication working together, for example, a written text and a visual sign

**Narrative**   A narrative is a story. The term is also used to describe the way a story is told

**Narrator, narratee**   The narrator is the person in a text who appears to be addressing the reader. The narratee is the implied reader of a text, whose identity is built up by a series of assumptions that are made about the reader

**Paralanguage**  Aspects of language which work alongside verbal language, such as body posture and facial expression

**Pragmatics**  The way meanings in texts, written or spoken, can work beyond the apparent surface meaning

**Proper nouns**  Proper nouns are the names of people, places, etc. which are usually written with a capital letter

**Prosodics**  Prosodic features refer to aspects of sound such as pitch, volume and tempo

**Prototype**  Psychologists call the idealised form of something a prototype. It represents the 'best' example of an object

**Register**  This is where the language used reflects the context and genre

**Repertoire**  A range of language types that an individual can use

**Represented talk**  Talk that is fictional rather than 'real' talk

**Rhetorical question**  A rhetorical question is a question which is asked, but without the expectation of a reply

**Script**  A term taken from psychology which suggests certain human interactions will take certain forms

**Semantics/semantic field**  Semantics refers to the study of linguistic meaning. A semantic field is a group of words which are related in meaning as a result of being connected with a particular context of use. 'Shot', 'header', 'tackle', 'throw-in' are all connected with the semantic field of football

**Semiotics**  Communication by means of signs and symbols

**Sign/signifier/signified**  In semiotics, the term 'sign' means 'something that has significance'. The sign itself is termed the signifier, and what it communicates is known as the signified. So the sign of an apple could be a signifier for the signified meaning of something healthy

**Symbolism**  This involves association between things rather than direct reference

**Synonym**  Synonyms are words which have equivalent meanings

**Taboo**  Taboo language is language that is 'forbidden'

**Unmarked**  Whereas marked words indicate a specific category, unmarked words are 'normal' or 'neutral' in meaning. So, for example, 'steward' is unmarked but 'stewardess' is marked, suggesting a specifically female attendant